Icarus World Issues Series

Street Gangs
Gaining Turf, Losing Ground

Series Editors, Roger Rosen and Patra McSharry

THE ROSEN PUBLISHING GROUP, INC.
NEW YORK

Published in 1991 by The Rosen Publishing Group, Inc.
29 East 21st Street, New York, NY 10010

First Edition

Library of Congress Cataloging-in Publication Data

Street gangs : gaining turf, losing ground. -- 1st ed.
    p.   cm.   -- (Icarus world issues series)
    Includes bibliographical references and index.
    Summary: Essays, fiction, and photographs address different aspects of apartheid.
    ISBN 0-8239-1332-5 (hardcover)
              0-8239-1333-3 (paperback)
    1. Gangs. 2. Social groups   I. Series.
    DT1757.A62   1991
    302.3'4--dc20   91-22204
                                                           CIP
                                                           AC

CONTENTS

Introduction

Street Gangs: You've see them hanging out near abandoned buildings, waging war in movies, busted on the evening news. They're the broken clause in the social contract, the phenomenon we all shy away from as we intellectually and emotionally cross to the other side of the street.

Our third issue of *Icarus* takes you over the terrain of "them" and "us," the mind-set of both the disenfranchised and the embraced. If the universe of our investigations were so easily delineated, however, we'd be guilty of taking you slumming through the shantytowns and ghettos that serve as a breeding ground for so many of these gangs. Instead, we've left the air-conditioned buses and tour guides behind and asked our contributors to cross the mental and physical barriers on the street. What they've brought back is no less than a complex portrait of our social constructs shattered by poverty and despair into stilettos of hate. Society damages itself.

The nature of the damage has escalated into more outrageous and intolerable forms. The jump from carrying switchblades to toting submachine guns becomes as inevitable as the advances of each new generation of computer. How could it be otherwise given society's blessing on the inexorable progression toward "more"?

The Sharks and the Jets of "West Side Story" exhibit an innocence that is positively refreshing in light of the practices of the new corporate gangs that run the drug trade in Detroit with brutal efficiency. Marlon Brando in "The Wild Ones" was a safe embodiment of American rebellion and dissnt; his more sophisticated contemporary equivalents use cellular car phones and conform, albeit operating on the other side of the looking glass. Gangs today are less interested in turf and loyalty. They've gotten smart and hunkered down to the business of business. That's progress: and society suffers the singular anguish of being hoist with its own petard.

In this issue, Jack Willoughby's brilliant look at the traveling Vietnamese gangs is a particularly poignant testimony of a country reaping what it has sown. The unvarnished voices of Loca and James L., two gang members interviewed by author Elliott Currie, convey the odds stacked against kids struggling to emerge into a dignified conception of self. Pierre Venant's remarkable photographs record the brutality and vulnerability of the infamous LA gangs. William Kotzwinkle has written a story that focuses on a hungry homeless man and the simple, unspeakably wrenching despair of life on the street.

The United States, however, does not hold a monopoly on gangs and gang violence. Joe Joseph transports us to Tokyo to acquaint us with the Japanese *yakuza*; Luis Francia takes us through the dusty streets of Manila; Dmitrii Likhanov introduces us to gang leaders in Kazan and Tashkent; and Gerald Posner escorts us through the Walled City of Hong Kong, the citadel of the Triads. From South Africa, Chris Ledochowski draws the connection between apartheid policy and the emergence of the *skollie* gangs, and James Campbell shares his own history as a Billy Boy in Glasgow.

These authors convey the universality of the condition of the outsider trying to get in. Their coverage does not fail to capture the specifics of lives that have been forged on the indigenous anvil of neglect, oppression, and sometimes simple ignorance.

Roger Rosen
Editor

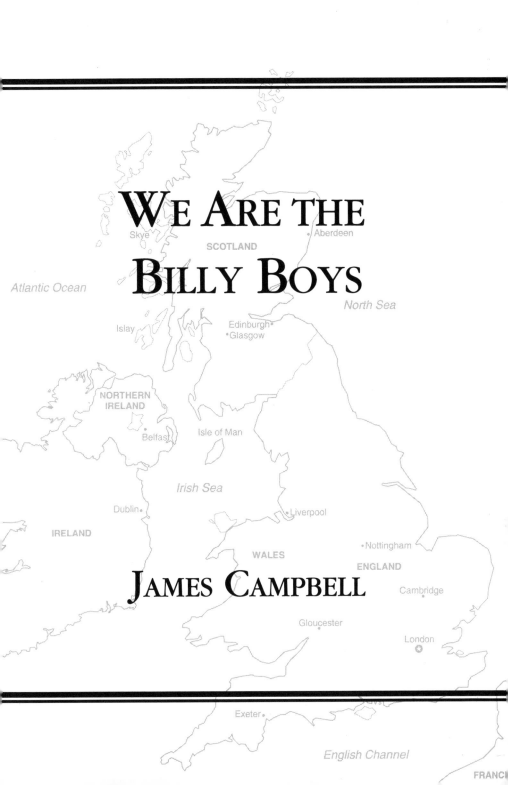

WE ARE THE
BILLY BOYS

JAMES CAMPBELL

James Campbell was born in Glasgow, Scotland, in 1951. He quit school at fifteen and worked for three years as a printer's apprentice before going "on the road," traveling through Europe to Turkey, Israel, and North Africa.

In 1978, Mr. Campbell started editing a literary magazine, the *New Edinburgh Review*, whose contributors included James Baldwin, Henry Miller, William Burroughs, and most of the leading Scottish writers. He is the author of three books: *Invisible Country: A Journey through Scotland; Gate Fever: Voices from a Prison;* and most recently, *Talking at the Gates: A Life of James Baldwin.*

Mr. Campbell currently works as an editor at the *Times Literary Supplement* and is a regular contributor to a number of newspapers and periodicals, including the *Sunday Times of London*, the *London Review of Books*, and *Grand Street*. He lives in London.

This is 1965. The Billy Boys are rampant, triumphant, again. We've spent the afternoon inside a football [soccer] stadium in an industrial town near Glasgow. Our voices are high and rasping, our faces sunny with victory. And now comes the part we relish most: We are striding—all of a sudden stampeding—through the mean small-town center. Men and women, boys and girls, dogs and cats, all get out of our way. At intervals of about five minutes a song lifts our heads into the air:

(To the tune of "Marching through Georgia")

Hello! Hello!
We are the Billy Boys.
Hello! Hello!
You'll hear us by our noise.
We're up to our knees in Fenian blood,
Surrender or you'll die!
For we are the Brigton Billy Boys.

Ten or fifteen of us cram into a café, drink Coca-Cola through straws, make dirty puns to the waitress about our "coacks," and leave without paying. Outside, a sly smile on his fat lips, Shorty elbows me in the ribs and, as if revealing something of value, slowly slides his fist out of his coat pocket. It's clutching a Coca-Cola bottle. Shorty laughs. He knows he holds the torch. He swivels and hurls the bottle through the plate-glass window of the café. In the confusion of laughter and swearing someone shouts "Fuggin polis!" and everyone takes off in a run.

Hello! Hello!
We are the Billy Boys.

Sideways down a railway embankment, stumbling down to the even bed in Cuban heels, jogging along the track toward the bridge up ahead.

— Watch oot fur a train.
— Fugga train. We *are* the Billy Boys!

Then it's up the steep embankment again, aided by handfuls of gravel and weeds. Shorty needs a shove from below to help him over the iron railings at the top. From the bridge we can look down on railway track stretching back 500 yards without seeing a single policeman. There is a pause, an instant's idle depression, when nothing happens. It's one of those moments when everyone is waiting for someone else to do or say the thing that will carry it all further, lift the high a foot higher . . . And suddenly there—as if the film has been spliced and a new scene is beginning before the last one has ended—there they are. The other side. Dirty rotten Fenian bastards.

Shorty speaks, to test the air, to see if his breath comes out solid. It doesn't. They sense his fear before he knows he has it himself. They spit back.

—Youse getoota here.
—Better no come the funny man aroon here.
—Better get tae fug.

One of them has a knife, about four inches long. He is a quiet one. He hasn't spoken yet and neither have I (Shorty does all our talking), but when I see the knife in his hand I shuffle like a boxer and step toward him. I feel the others freeze behind me. A moment's hesitation on his side means humiliation and already a victory for me.

—Come on ya
dirty

rotten
Fenian BASTAAARDD

Turning to run, he drops his knife. As I stoop to pick it up, he is already haring across a pitch of waste ground. Losing no more than a yard or two, I hound after him.

I can well imagine the outbreak of panic that the sight of us, swarming through the town or one of Glasgow's suburbs, ten or twenty-strong, brought to the breasts of respectable, middle-class citizens. A panic both moral and physical, for while the sudden presence of the mob on an otherwise quiet thoroughfare might cause people fear, it also outraged their sense of propriety that boys should behave in this way. Their decency was despoiled by our barbarity. We used their neat gardens as litter-bins and toilets. And if they were shocked, that was what we wanted; their fury was our reward; we reveled in being "mental" (a favorite word) and pissing in front of their lace curtains.

"Get back off to where you belong," a brave housewife or an elderly man would shout, waving an angry hand as if that could sweep us back down into the burrows and dank warrens of Glasgow's worst slums.

We did not see ourselves as rats, or rodents of any other kind. We were lions looking for Christians. Our Colosseum was the football stadium we had just left, in whichever town in depressed central Scotland the match was taking place that week—Motherwell, Paisley, Kilmarnock, Stirling, or Glasgow itself.

The biggest fixture on the calendar is the game between Glasgow's two leading teams, Rangers and Celtic. This takes place about three times a year and is among the city's major events. The meeting of these two teams is not just a football match: It symbolizes the ancient religious opposition in Scotland between Protestants and Catholics,

5

those loyal to the Crown and those who look instead to
Rome and the Vatican. Our team is Rangers, the
Protestants, dressed in royal blue. Until recently, in all the
120 years of Rangers history, the club had never signed a
Catholic player. No matter that he was the greatest wizard
the sport could produce—if his name was Liam or Daniel,
or Patrick or Bernard, or Dominic or Vincent, he would not
play for Rangers. (When in 1989 Rangers at last took a
Catholic into their ranks, he needed police protection on
his home, and thousands of Rangers supporters burnt their
season tickets.) The Catholics' club is Celtic, whose
emblem is the Irish shamrock and who dress in green—
they are RCs, dans, papes, timmalloys, cannibals, dirty-
rotten-Fenian-bastards. They are our sworn enemies, as
decreed by church and history.

Picture a sports stadium, the largest in Europe, filled to
the brim with 150,000 people—the population of an
ordinary town. They have congregated to watch Rangers
play Celtic in the annual Cup Final. At the entry onto the
grass pitch below of the two teams, led by their captains,
in bright, bright blue and emerald-green, all the feelings
the crowd can expectorate are released into the smoke-
and-beer-soured air: blind devotion to their team and
bigoted hatred of the others, mixed with bitterness
directed at themselves for their own work-and-drink-
dominated lives.

The victors will carry off the 100-year-old silver Scottish
Cup, with the team's name and the date inscribed. Each
one of its 75,000 supporters will settle down comfortably
tonight remembering how the captain raised the trophy
above his head; each will revel in the part he played
personally in the victory.

To the losers, despondency. The repetitive tedium of
their daily lives could have been vindicated but instead
has been mocked. They will cry over their beer and be
drunk by early evening. Some will beat out their misery on

their wives, some on each other. There will be fistfights and stabbings and razor-slashings, probably a murder or two.

Football in Scotland isn't a matter of life and death, a famous team-manager once said: It's more important than that.

It all goes back to a real battle, fought by real armies, three hundred years ago. At the end of the seventeenth century Scotland and England, though largely Protestant, were ruled by a Catholic king, James VII. When a Protestant outsider, William of Orange from the Netherlands, challenged the throne, he gained the immediate support of the masses. The decisive battle was fought in Ireland in 1690, the Battle of the Boyne. The forces of William (King Billy) defeated those of the Catholic James, and Protestantism reigned supreme. "1690!" became the Protestant's victory medal and his war cry. It is today the only date that many Scots are able to identify in the history books.

The football teams came much later, though the cause they contested was basically the same one. Rangers Football Club was founded in 1872, Celtic fifteen years on as a charity organization set up by priests to absorb the energies of poor Catholic boys. The Battle of the Boyne was revived to be fought again three or four times every year. The football-religion was thus established, and the slogan "1690!" is still the Rangers war cry.

Our song, "We are the Billy Boys," is the unofficial anthem of Glasgow Rangers. The original Brigton Billy Boys were a gang of the 1920s and '30s, the first to be identified at one and the same time with the soccer club and the Protestant cause, binding the two together in a cult of violence. Glasgow in the 1930s was notorious for razor gangs and razor kings, and the Billy Boys attained immortality by being the first to take up arms in the cause of the football-religion. They got their name from the district they came from, Bridgeton ("Brigton"), and from their leader, Billy Fullerton—King Billy II. On Saturdays they stood behind the Rangers goal in the huge, echoing stadium and bawled taunts and slogans at Irish Catholics all afternoon—no matter that it so happened the team Rangers were playing that week was, like them, made up entirely of Protestants.

King Billy Fullerton was an unrepentant thug (he later drummed up support for the British Fascists during World War II), as were most of his gang, but many otherwise peaceable Glaswegian Protestants followed his example when it came to Saturday afternoons. You didn't need to have a propensity for violence, or a strong dislike of Catholics, to take your place with the Billy Boys on the terraces of the football grounds. You sang the hymns of the football-religion—"We're up to our knees in Fenian blood"—even if you could say that some of your best friends were Fenians.

The Catholic presence was exorcised from Scotland with the removal of James VII. There were at one time more anti-Catholic societies in Glasgow than actual Catholics (in the 1790s the count was forty-three societies to thirty-nine Catholic citizens). But during the famine years of the 1840s starving Catholic families came in droves from the potato fields of southern Ireland to the industrial heartland of Scotland. In the view of the polite Glasgow citizenry, they appeared dirty, coarse, ill-educated; to the less refined they posed a threat, since they were prepared to work cheaply. To all, equally, their religion was unwelcome. The deep stain that soils the Catholic heart in Protestant eyes—from King William of Orange to King Billy of Brigton to the Billy Boys of today—will not budge.

The street where I grew up in Glasgow in the 1950s was almost totally Protestant, and belief in the base nature of

Catholics was firm. For example, we believed that in Catholic schools more time was devoted to religious indoctrination than to the basics of real life, sums and spelling; to the austere Protestant mind, liberated from worship of graven images by Martin Luther, the thought was revolting. We believed that their priests operated as a secret police force, visiting people's homes and enforcing attendance at chapel, urging the women to have more and more babies (Catholic families were always larger than ours) so that Rome could eventually take over Scotland and the world.

Mixed marriage between the two sects was rare in Glasgow. The Protestant partner was forced to swear before the priest that the (numerous) children would be brought up as Catholics. Had a Protestant girl decided to marry a Jew or a Hindu, her parents would most likely have raised an eyebrow and offered a sage word of advice about the wisdom of sticking to "your own kind." But to think of marrying a pape! Splits have been caused in families over this that have never been repaired, and the reasonable appeal that Catholics are, after all, our fellow Christians has never helped prevent one.

Suspicion bred superstition. Catholics did not eat meat on Fridays, only fish; therefore "fish on a Friday" was strictly off the Protestant menu. No one ever set foot inside a Catholic church, and few would venture into Catholics' living rooms for fear of being tainted by their beliefs. The crucifixes hanging round their necks and on their bedroom walls, with representations of the agonized Christ, hinted at a Satanic pleasure in cruelty and pain. Law-abiding Protestants were convinced that the motive behind the Catholic's weekly visit to the confessional was that it justified his criminality: The Catholic sinned, confessed to the priest, and was then free to sin again.

We had created a tribal "other": alien (Rome and Ireland combined), lawless, primitive, guilty of unrestricted

9

breeding, and a slave to heathen ritual. To seven- and eight-year-old children he was a threat, a bogeyman, and there was virtue in resisting him. We linked arms for the first time and marched homeward through the streets after school, in short trousers and smartly brushed blazers, on toward the banks of the glorious Boyne, singing

> We're up to our knees in Fenian blood,
> Surrender or you'll die!
> For we are the Brigton Billy Boys.

*   *   *

Seven years on, in 1965, I could imagine how the people felt at the sight of our raggle-taggle bunch in their polite streets on a Saturday after the match. For while I was at Shorty's side—*Aye Ready!*—I could also see myself through the eyes of those folk we so gleefully terrorized, my parents' eyes.

All of the Billy Boys but me came from the lowest zone of the working class and lived in the Gorbals slums. It was the wrong part of town as far as our family was concerned—my mother and father had devoted their energies to climbing out of there in the years before we were born—but the right part for me. Something must have been carried over in the genes from past days, for from the time I first found myself in the Gorbals I felt at home. There was a kind of life in those long, long streets of high brown tenements, where the women hung out of windows gossiping all day long and families slept three to a bed, that was missing where we lived, half-an-hour's walk away. Girls down in the Gorbals said things that put your hair on end. Boys grew into men quickly and were married and settled into a life of gambling, drink, and petty crime by the time they were twenty.

So the boy on the railway bridge, when he pulled out

his knife so nervously that I had no hesitation in challenging him, was giving me the opportunity to prove myself. When I took a step toward him, I was walking out of one world—parents, school, "getting on"—into another, the offensive, hilarious, generous, erotic world of the Gorbals.

He ran as fast as he could across the waste ground, with me hard behind. The knife was now in my hand. It had cost me a yard or more, but I would have caught him had I not suddenly poled over like a felled tree and hit the ground with my face. I thought I had tripped. Then I thought his mates had got me. I rolled over and looked up and saw a giant policeman standing above me. He was staring at the knife, which was still in my hand. I started spouting explanations and surrendered it. He picked me up, shook me about a bit, and asked for my name and where I lived. All the details I gave him he wrote down. He told me to go to the railway station and get out of town and to think myself lucky I wasn't spending the night in jail.

I started to walk away. I had given a false name and address anyway, so I felt as if I had the last laugh. On the way down to the station, over the now-deserted bridge, I kept an eye out for Shorty and the others, but they were nowhere to be seen. Probably they were already traveling home, having seen enough of a policeman's boots. On the train back to Glasgow I fell in with another crowd, and we spent the journey recounting tales of our exploits, talking nonstop over one another, boasting and singing football songs, every so often punctuated by the cry of "1690!"

The date meant more to me when I was a child of seven than when I was a gang member of fourteen, by which time the cause was stronger on our lips than in our hearts. It means nothing to me now, emotionally speaking, though few events in the past 300 years have had as much influence on the place I come from and the people who live in it as the arrival of William of Orange from the Netherlands, King Billy, and his defeat of King James on the banks of the Boyne.

A long time after I had left the Billy Boys behind and lost my all-consuming interest in the weekly fortunes of Glasgow Rangers, I made a surprising discovery. Our loyal Protestant family was actually Popish at the source. Sixty years earlier we hadn't been Billies at all—we had been Fenians. But for an unusual action on my grandparents' part, that is what we would have remained. I myself would have been the very "other" whom we as children had reviled.

My father's father was a Catholic. At the beginning of the century he and his bride had made one of those rare mixed marriages and had brought up the first of many children as the priest demanded. But then they switched sides—mid-match, as it were—and began sending the younger ones to a Protestant school. No formal declaration was required. It would have been enough for the Protestant half of the union—my grandmother—to seek an interview with a Church of Scotland minister and then the headmaster of the local school. The family's Catholic identity was effectively ditched at the side of the road from Rome.

Had this information come to light while I was a small boy, it would have caused confusion and doubtless some pain. As things turned out, the young man who had gloried in being one of Us could treat with ironic amusement the word that he was actually one of Them.

THE DUSTY REALM

OF BAGONG BARRIO

LUIS FRANCIA

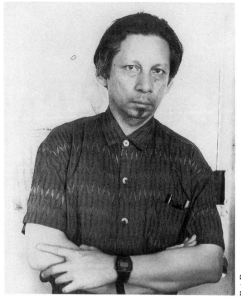

Pat Roque

Born and raised in Manila, Luis H. Francia now lives in New York City. He is a poet, critic, and free-lance writer. Mr. Francia is the author of *The Arctic Archipelago & Other Poems*, and coauthor of *Her Beauty Likes Me Well*. He also wrote the Philippines section for the current *Fodor's Southeast Asia Guide*. His forthcoming book—*Brown River, White Ocean: An Anthology of 20th Century Philippine Literature in English*, will be published next year by Rutgers University Press.

Mr. Francia's work has been featured in *Asiaweek*, *In These Times*, *Linden Lane*, *The Literary Review*, *Village Voice*, and other publications. In 1978 he received the Palanca Memorial Award for Poetry.

Mr. Francia has traveled widely throughout the Philippines and is currently at work on a book about that country.

In the dry season, when the heat is as fierce as a rabid dog, dust reigns supreme in Bagong Barrio, or New Town. It is everywhere, draining the colors even from the sparse greenery and contributing to the obvious irony that in New Town everything—and everyone—looks old. Now a crowded settlement that is home turf to about 100,000 people, BB (as the locals call it) began as a squatter colony in 1970. Shanties line the roads, built with scrap iron, discarded pieces of wood, cardboard, and prayer. Erected right beside the refuse-filled canals that flank the roads, these jerry-built homes are little more than ovens in the summer and meager shelters at the height of the monsoon season. Their inhabitants live a great deal of their waking lives on the street, where there is air—polluted though it may be—and light. From the cab I can see unkempt grimy kids everywhere, playing on the road or in the narrow dark alleyways that divide the shanties into rows. Privacy here is as abstract a notion as snow in Alaska.

Bert is the young and cheerful taxi driver who is taking me to Our Virgin of Lourdes, the parish church, where I am to meet Tatang Joseph, a church worker who knows some local gang members. Bert expertly wends his way through the knots of kids and the dogs that loll about. The road itself is one of the few paved in the barrio. It's easy to see why: A number of garment factories, whose products wind up in the showrooms of the West, line the avenue. Bert makes his living mainly by ferrying lovesick couples from the nearby national highway to the several motels (owned, Bert tells me, by the factory owners) within BB where they can spend a few hours of amorous play in air-conditioned comfort. Indeed, in this impossible heat lovemaking can be only an act of fortitude and grunty perspiration.

Behind the shacks are sturdier wooden houses rendered

drab by dust and dark clouds of exhaust from the incessant vehicular traffic. Intermittently and usually close to the factories appear the high-walled expensive concrete residences of the factory owners, but even these homes, guarded as they are by ubiquitous blue-uniformed security men, are not spared the ministrations of dust. The owners are extravagantly rich and, in a reminder that BB exists in some kind of time warp, generally act like medieval lords. The cops and the local politicians are beholden to them, the neighborhood hoods know better than to scale their walls, and certain neighborhood labor organizers (or "subversives" as they're jeeringly labeled by right-wingers) have been known to disappear. With laws on wages and safe working conditions rarely enforced, the crafty entrepreneurs reap tremendous profits.

I ask Bert about gangs in the neighborhood. He tells me there are a few but not as many as before. In 1970, he says, when Bagong Barrio began its turbulent life, there were numerous violent quarrels over turf. The police rarely intervened, partly out of fear and partly out of indifference. For the civil authorities, undermined by endemic corruption and overwhelmed by meager budgets and a barely existing social service structure, the squatters were—and are—a pain in the ass. And so the gangs filled a vacuum, providing some kind of discernible hierarchy, a leadership, rough as it was, to solve disputes and keep order, one largely based on heads being cracked.

Nowadays turf questions have been more or less settled, each gang with its own fiefdom, large or small depending on the gang's size and the savoir faire, as well as political connections, of its leaders. Gang wars still flare up, but not as frequently. The bosses try to avoid bloody conflict as much as possible. It doesn't benefit either side, decimates their ranks, and may make them fair prey for upstart gangs. Besides, with the factories springing up—the poor here provide a plentiful and cheap pool of labor—there has been a police and military presence in the area. And a dose of upward mobility for a few relatively fortunate families. But BB still exists as an aggregation of hard-strapped neighborhoods greater than the whole. Into many of them the stranger is well advised not to venture.

Every neighborhood in Manila—rich, middle class, working class, or dirt poor—has its own gangs. I remember growing up in a middle-class neighborhood that had two teenage gangs, the AXIS and the ALLIED gangs, controlling separate parts of the area. I belonged to neither but had friends among the ALLIED gang, which was closer to our home. I remember Eddie and Jimmy, the ALLIED leaders, imitating Jimmy Dean's swagger and that of movie-screen gangs, riding around in their parents' cars, hair slicked back, getting drunk a lot. There were frequent fights between the two gangs, but as I recall none of them ever ended in anyone's death, though there were a lot of bloody noses and broken ribs. A far cry from the deadlier duels between today's gangs.

There are, of course, much larger and more powerful gangs. The astutely cynical say that the worst gangs are the patronage politicians or, in street parlance, *trapos*, literally meaning "rags." *Trapos* are often warlords, with small armies of well-armed foot soldiers. They use public office to enrich themselves and a chosen cabal, to soak up money as it were. In the country's recent history, Marcos and his cronies are the supreme example. At the bottom of the social spectrum are the runaways, the street kids. Manila being the Philippines' largest city has the most: The official count is 75,000, although almost everyone agrees that the real figure is much higher. Seeking escape from abusive parents or parents who can no longer provide sustenance, much less education, the kids, tough and worldly before their time, have their own gangs but are nevertheless fair prey for pimps and drug pushers. In the predatory worlds of Manila, too many wind up as drug addicts or toys for pedophiles.

In between the *trapos* and the street kids is a whole hierarchy. There are the *barkadas*, loosely organized, basically harmless groups of friends whose main aim is to party; the *istambays* or unemployed neighborhood toughs, whose raison d'être is drinking and mauling passersby; district gangs, whose turf includes several neighborhoods and whose membership is young and from all social classes; gangs based on regional affiliation; and the specialized criminal gangs like the *akyat bahay* (porch climbers) and the purse snatchers. There are even gangs made up of ex-military personnel who specialize in car theft and bank robbery. But the most feared gangs are the criminal *sindicatos*, older, much wealthier, and with ties to the establishment. Like their counterparts in other countries (the Triads in Hong Kong, the *yakuza* in Japan), the *sindicatos* control such lucrative enterprises as gambling, smuggling, money laundering, prostitution, and the black market in foreign currency.

In the context of both Philippine culture and history, highly tribalistic in nature and with loyalties forged on the basis of personal ties and kinship, the rise (and fall) of gangs is a natural phenomenon, as natural as the palm trees and the bougainvillea dotting the countryside. The recorded, mainly colonial, history of this country is rife with references to peasant-based secret societies, founded as a counterweight to the oppressive thrust of the elitist, oligarchical establishment. These societies were a way for the masses to get their own, even if it meant bloody insurrections.

The dusty realm of Bagong Barrio can be seen as a microcosm of Philippine society, from the jarring day-and-night contrasts between rich and poor and the labyrinthine network of social and familial relationships, to its politics and gangs. BB has at least four well-known street gangs. Two are criminal, the Commandos and the Sputniks, most of whose members are middle-aged, hardened criminals. The leaders of both have fearsome reputations as killers, and local folks steer clear of any entanglements with the gangs. Tatang Joseph, my source, says it's easy to find the two bosses but that, as far as he knows, neither one has ever spent substantial time behind bars. They have friends among the police, who are not exactly paragons of civic virtue (on their meager salaries, no one expects them to be). On the street the two bosses are known to detest each other, but neither goes "hunting"—street parlance for stalking and gunning down your enemy. They have a tenuous live-and-let-live arrangement.

The other well-known BB gangs are AKHRO and ZEAL, made up mainly of young men in their mid- to late teens and early twenties. For the most part they're unemployed or underemployed; i.e., they work as casual laborers for the factories for periods of up to six months, then are laid off before they can legally claim benefits as regular employees. In many ways mirror images of the Commandos and Sputniks, AKHROns and ZEALots are not fond of one another and jealously guard their turfs. Although their intended aim is not criminal activity, they do in fact countenance, if not encourage, lawbreaking. No one questions you if you suddenly sport a brand-new watch or flash some bucks. The more ambitious members of the two street gangs often run errands for the Commandos or the Sputniks, take part in petty crimes, and even take a fall. Like rivers that depend on different tributaries for their existence, the Commandos and Sputniks recruit from the ranks of AKHRO and ZEAL. I spent some time talking to three ZEAL members in BB and emerged with a portrait of a gang that is fairly typical in slum neighborhoods.

Thirty-year-old mustachioed Narding A. founded ZEAL when he was fourteen years old, to protect himself and his friends from the bullies at the local high school who made their lives miserable. Married, with one child, Narding smiles easily. On weekends he works as a bouncer at a local disco that doubles on weekdays as an arena for cockfights. It sounds like a wild place. Its owner undoubtedly pays off the cops, as cockfighting is illegal. Narding does not have a bouncer's bulk, but he knows all the toughs in the area and has friends among the cops, many of whom once belonged to ZEAL. Most patrons know better than to give Narding trouble.

He claims that ZEAL originated in California in 1931. In 1975 he met a Filipino-American member who was visiting and who gave him a license to establish a Philippines counterpart. Is this a real story, or apocryphal? Was the Filipino-American pulling Narding's leg? No matter: ZEAL is very real.

We are in his small, concrete house set a little apart from a cluster of wooden houses at the end of a dirt road on the bank of a narrow polluted creek. Across the creek we can see the outskirts of Valenzuela, a town in Bulacan, the province that abuts the northern end of Metro Manila. Narding lives where he lives for tactical reasons. To get to his place from the main road, Tatang and I have to park our borrowed jeepney (an old World War II army vehicle converted to civilian use) and start walking toward Narding's house. We can feel the gaze of several men hanging out in front of the *sari-sari* (a poor man's version of a general store). They watch us coolly, carefully. By the time we reach the cluster of ramshackle houses we have been noted and appraised by the neighbors who act as Narding's praetorian guard. (On occasion members of other gangs have mistakenly walked in here and wound up badly beaten.) The creek provides a handy escape route. He can leap into it from his kitchen window and cross to the other side.

When we near the men, Tatang smiles and asks for Narding, though he knows where Narding lives as he has been here before. It is to allay the young men's suspicions and acknowledge their existence. In a poor hardscrabble neighborhood like BB, codes of behavior may be unwritten but they're strictly observed. A perceived snub, an ill-timed look, a brusque tone can mean a knife in the gut or a bottle smashed on one's head. I smile with Tatang, my notebook clearly in hand so they can see (I hope) that I'm one of those opinionated fools, a writer. They nod and let us pass.

Narding's living room is almost devoid of furniture except for a raised platform that doubles as a place to sit, although there are benches around two sides. Through a wide window facing the creek are wafted the sickly sweet smells of rotten garbage and stagnant water. Still, a breeze comes through, providing a significant measure of relief. Narding is bright and clever, a glint in his eyes. "*Ako'y taong kalsada*" (I am a man of the streets), he declares with a grin, and I sense right away that he's a natural politician. He admits having political ambitions and says he may run for barrio captain (something like a city councillor) in the next district elections.

He already has a significant constituency in ZEAL, whose membership, according to him, is 20,000 in the metropolitan area, mostly among working-class students in the university belt, a district in downtown Manila where several universities are located. Each campus has its own ZEAL chapter, presided over by a president. All the presidents in turn report periodically to Narding. But ZEAL's main base is here in Bagong Barrio, around Araneta University and Araneta Subdivision, a middle-class housing area. (Most real estate around the area

21

belongs to the Araneta clan, a powerful wealthy family.) He calls ZEAL a "fraternity gang," but as a frat its activities would make those of its American counterpart seem like the genteel goings-on of an association of retired accountants. Especially in a tough neighborhood like Bagong Barrio, ZEAL is closer to a teenage gang from Harlem. While its base of recruitment is the student population, its extracurricular life is that of a street gang. ZEAL has its own passwords and a hand signal, a clenched fist but with the thumb and the index and small fingers upright. I realize that except for the thumb it's the cuckold's sign. The more senior members also sport round scar tissue at the back of their palms, the result of a red-hot peso coin branding the flesh. Narding's scar tissue is a large callused lump of flesh.

In ZEAL's early days Narding reveled in his role as commanding general. "We were all spoiling for a fight, any fight. Any gang attacked any of our members, and we'd pay them back in kind." According to gang codes, however, there were (and still are) rules to follow, especially when it came to a "rumble," or armed show-down. The number of members each side brought didn't matter as long as the combatants were in the open. The kind of weapons brought was to be agreed upon in advance. But before fighting erupted, the two leaders would try to talk out their differences and determine if there were another way to settle the grievance in question. Narding laughs. Such rules were quickly dispensed with when hotheads on both sides started trading insults. For all his love of a fight, Narding says he always tried to follow the rules. It was always the other side, according to him, that broke the unwritten code. I take this with a grain of salt: No gang will ever admit to breaking the code. And I sense that, politician that he is, Narding embellishes his accounts from time to time.

He tells me with some braggadocio—crows might be a better word—that once the fight began he would keep moving forward, lashing out with a club, oblivious to blows. He describes gang members (whether his or someone else's) as "rarely individually brave but once you start your foray, they follow." He never looked back until he was knocked out or the other side fled. "There were times when I just woke up in the hospital."

Some rumbles end in death. Narding himself has been accused of murder. In one gang war some years ago (he won't say when), an opposing gang member was killed— first shot, then hacked. That was in retribution, he says, for one of his own having been killed treacherously as the two sides faced off. He's vague if it was indeed he. "I'm the leader so it was me they blamed, it was me the cops were after. I hid and so they picked up my father and put him in jail. I had to give myself up." He and ZEAL managed to get off the hook by settling with the victim's family for P42,000, an insignificant sum in dollars but a huge sum for BB. (Later, I find out from someone else that Narding did some time behind bars. It's a touchy issue with him.) In a poor community like BB, the economic realities of life far outweigh abstract notions of justice. A man languishing in jail provides no income and, as he lives, is little solace to the victim's family. There are, after all, other ways of evening the score. Take the money when you can and revenge later on.

AKHROns are the ZEALots' mortal enemies. Narding describes them as a "traitorous bunch, drug addicts, *barumbados* (roughnecks), they'll jump you when you're alone." He used to go out with five or six gang members as bodyguards. I'm sure he has enemies, yet he claims he no longer goes about with an entourage. But that may be because he's been staying close to home lately. He does have an *alalay*, a 13-year-old. An *alalay* is a sure sign of status, a combination of gofer, ego booster, and court jester. The greater one's status, the more *alalays* one is likely to have.

In essence, an *alalay* is the ultimate groupie, a devout acolyte to the almost sacrosanct figure of his or her patron. The *alalay* and the patron have a remarkable symbiotic relationship, representing in crystalline fashion the classic gang relationship. In return for the *alalay's* many devotions, the patron/boss is expected to provide not so much for physical needs but status, protection, and above all, an idealized center around which the *alalay* revolves. Both give up significant amounts of privacy, but it is a tradeoff easily accepted. Narding seems quite comfortable having his teenaged *alalay* around, even when the matters under discussion may not concern the *alalay*. The kid is street savvy but nevertheless has an innocence I invariably find among Manila's street kids.

Most bigwigs in Manila society have *alalays*. The most visible, certainly best known, are those of the female movie stars, and the biggest star in terms of *alalays* is Nora Aunor. "La Aunor," as she is called, is a dark-skinned chanteuse-turned-actress (and a damned good one at that) and comes from a poor provincial family. That and the fact that she isn't a *mestiza* beauty—one with Caucasian features—are two reasons why millions of poor women with few physical role models go gaga over her. This explains why most of her several *alalays* are female. Her band of *alalays* is noted for its unflinching loyalty and the alacrity with which its members spring to her defense against any and all aspersions, real or imagined, cast by *alalays* of rival stars, especially those of Vilma Santos. The rivalry between the NORAns and the VILMAns is every bit as intense, though not bloody, as that between the AKHROns and the ZEALots.

The big problem nowadays with teenagers, as in other urban areas around the globe, is drugs. Here because

24

they're cheap, the drugs of choice are glue (Rugby is a favored brand), cough syrup (for the codeine) and shabu, a local version of crack. Glue is especially popular with street kids, as sniffing it dulls hunger pangs. Those members with drug habits often resort to theft and even extortion of money from students. Narding downplays drug use among his members, though clearly he doesn't like it. He has told the members, however, that no one is to attend meetings drunk or stoned.

On another equally hot and dusty day I hang out with Hermie V., a younger gang member. We're in a walled-in vacant lot about 10 meters from Narding's residence. It's where ZEAL members meet and plan their activities. The only structure in it is a shed in one corner, with a bed and some benches. I had thought that a large residence lay behind the walls. Instead, there are more than twenty fighting cocks tethered to small, triangular lean–tos. They strut about and crow loudly against the unforgiving sun. Hermie has some veterinary medical training and takes care of the sporting animals for a Chinese businessman, who lets the gang members use the lot for their meetings. As we talk, Narding drifts in and out, saying something about getting two teenage gang members for me to meet. At one point we spy him at the gate talking to two youngsters who look about seventeen or eighteen years old. I think, good, these must be the other two. But then they disappear hurriedly.

Hermie joined ZEAL during his high school years because "if you don't belong to a gang you're a helpless chick." He lives in another area of BB, called Reparo, his *baluarte* or bulwark, and acknowledges Narding as ZEAL's head. Hermie seems less impulsive than Narding. I ask him the secret of his having survived so many rumbles. He smiles slowly.

"I always showed up shortly after the rumble began. That way I can catch an opponent off guard."

"What weapon did you carry?"

"A 29."

"What's a 29?"

"A 29-inch *balisong*." A *balisong* is a native fan knife, and its stated length includes the folded handles as well as the blade. Still, a 29-inch balisong is a small lethal sword. Judging from his lack of visible scars, I'd say Hermie can do very well in a knife fight, a man to have on your side. I resist the temptation to ask if he has ever killed anyone.

His rear-guard tactics complement those.of Narding, who always leads the assault. Hermie describes a rumble as "like child's play. One side rushes, the other side retreats a bit, then counterattacks." He gestures toward his charges, "like fighting cocks." Hermie is quieter nowadays. Like Narding, he's married and has one kid. Like so many of his poor compatriots, he looks forward to leaving for the Middle East. He has gotten work in Saudi Arabia as a contract laborer and leaves in a month's time, perhaps escaping permanently the deadening life of the gang and of BB. He would have gone earlier, he says, but for the Gulf War. He's afraid of the loneliness in Saudi Arabia, and the xenophobia there—he has heard that the Saudis treat Filipinos badly. But the wages are good, there are no women or alcohol to be had, and he figures he can send enough money back for his wife to have a home built in BB.

Hermie and I reach a lull in our interview, and I'm wondering where Narding is. In a minute he appears. The two youngsters he was with earlier, both gang members, are in trouble. They have "dognapped," that is, stolen someone's dog, not for ransom but so they can prepare a poor man's viand they call *azucena*, a favorite dish to accompany hard drinking in squatter areas. The pet's owner has turned to Narding, who has promised to help.

He's hiding the two teens and persuading them to give up the dog. This show of neighborliness is born not out of altruism but out of the need to show that he's truly in command. If gang members were to start victimizing households in their own district, Narding would lose his power base and, worse, face.

He apologizes for not being with us, but Tatang Joseph and I tell him not to worry. We take our leave, and once on the main road Tatang asks me if I wish to see the grounds where ZEAL holds its hazings and where the rumbles between the gangs take place. I nod and we proceed to a trail that leads from the road and disappears behind some broken walls, taking us to a grassy ridged knoll. It is a wide, windswept place, with a drop of about 30 feet on one side. The field is at the back of the university, far from prying eyes and perfect for gang wars. One end of the trail leads to the rear of the university campus, which turns out to be depressingly shabby. We cross and enter and exit through some buildings. The walls have ZEAL and AKHRO emblazoned in white. We leave the campus through a break in one wall (I realize that most of the walls in the area have gaps that conveniently serve as passageways) and emerge in another section of BB, equally poor, equally dusty. As I follow Tatang through the neighborhoods, he points out which ones are ZEAL turfs and which ones, AKHRO's. I get the feeling that there are more conflicts between the two gangs than Narding is willing to admit.

The third ZEALot I hang out with is a handsome, neatly dressed seventeen-year-old, Samson D. Like Hermie, Samson joined ZEAL three years ago for protection against other gangs. It is he who gives me a good picture of ZEAL's initiation rites, and especially of the hazing. I had asked Narding about it, but he spoke only in a vague way.

Initiation into ZEAL is a three-step process, culminating in the applicant's being hazed. (Sometimes the beating administered by the frat gangs turns fatal. A month before I met Narding several members of a prominent private law school frat gang were charged with homicide: An applicant, an only son, had been hazed to death. The incident occupied the front pages for weeks.) The first step is desultory enough: interrogation by certain members who must be addressed as "Master." A Master can ask the applicant anything about his life. He is also entitled to slap the applicant if he thinks he's not being given enough respect.

The second stage is when it becomes interesting. The applicant is blindfolded and made to kneel with arms outstretched on either side. He is also given a new name; in Samson's case, Nognog. He is interrogated further, but this time as he replies his outstretched arms are continuously struck by other members. Samson/Nognog remembers collapsing to the floor several times. Each time he is allowed to recover and rest a few minutes before the process is resumed.

Next he is made to stand with his arms behind his head while he is "paddled"; that is, each member present is allowed to hit the applicant seven times with a short paddle anywhere except on the face and genitals. (At Samson's hazing, there were seventeen masters present, who administered a total of 119 paddle blows.) Then, to test his concentration, he is asked to grip a bottle between his legs, a procedure called "sandwich," and count to a hundred as a Master on either side hits or kicks him or whips him with a belt. If he misses a beat he is forced to begin again from one. Finally comes the "Indian Run": a gauntlet which the applicant must run twice as he is buffeted by blows from fists and paddles and belts. Before he begins his run he has to declare, "I love Narding A." At the end, Samson/Nognog says, "you're crawling, bruised all over, your arms swollen, you don't know which end is up." Samson had to be carried to the gang hideout, where he stayed until he recovered.

Samson has had his share of rumbles. The favored weapons are knives, iron rods, and homemade pillboxes. The latter are vicious things stuffed with gunpowder, shards of glass, and nails. They can make a person look like freshly cut meat. Some gang members who are cops' sons (many BB cops grew up as ZEAL members) pack guns, which range from a .45 caliber pistol to an M-16. Samson realizes, however, that there is really no future with ZEAL. He intones matter-of-factly, "I've seen so many of my gang friends destroyed by drugs or injured in rumbles. It's a world that is dangerously small."

Having recently been involved in some programs of Our Virgin of Lourdes parish church, Samson intends to quit ZEAL and continue with his studies—he finishes high school next year—unlike Narding and Hermie, both of whom dropped out of Araneta University. He knows that if he doesn't do it soon he may find it impossible, not because the gang won't let him, but because the protective cushion a gang like ZEAL offers its members, though ultimately illusory, can be addictive. In the harsh cul-de-sac life of Bagong Barrio, the support offered by a peer group is a seductive siren call. The irony is that in the end gang life itself becomes an even narrower cul-de-sac.

Of the three, the gang founder and leader Narding has the least prospects of transcending gang life. Although he has modest political ambitions, it is difficult to see how he will realize them. He himself is disillusioned with politics. He speaks bitterly of being used by the local pols during election campaigns, only to be conveniently forgotten once the voting is over. To him, there is no difference between the Marcos-era pols and those flourishing under

President Corazon Aquino. Still, a politician's life represents a concrete aim and a leap, given the current state of Philippines politics, into ultimate ganghood. Narding, I think, would do well in the public arena.

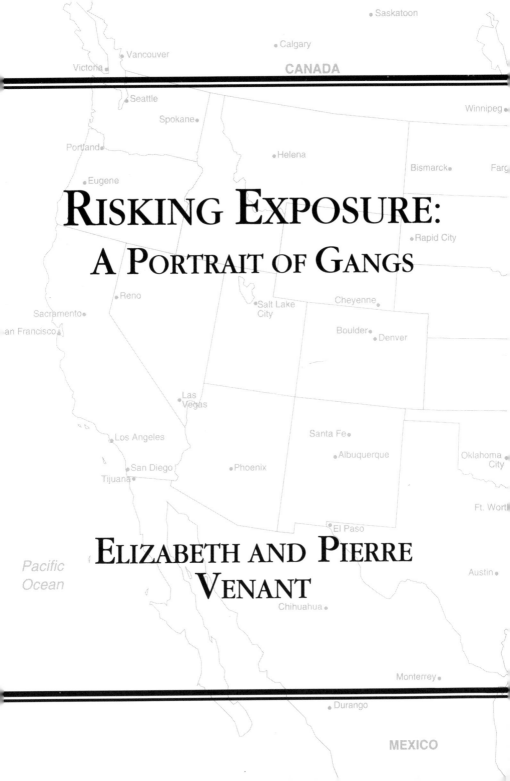

RISKING EXPOSURE:
A PORTRAIT OF GANGS

ELIZABETH AND PIERRE
VENANT

Elizabeth Venant is a senior writer for the *Los Angeles Times*, specializing in social issues, profiles, and trends of national significance. A journalist and editor for twenty years, Mrs. Venant has written for the *International Herald Tribune* in Paris, *Time*, and *Connoisseur*, and has worked on the staff of Reuters Information Services.

She lives in Los Angeles with her husband, Pierre Venant.

Pierre J. J. Venant learned photography from his father, one of the pioneers of portrait photography. He served as an army photographer during the Algerian War and later worked as a news photographer for *France Soir*. Mr. Venant moved to the United States in 1968 and worked as a fashion photographer. Later, he opened his own studio.

Mr. Venant is based in Los Angeles, where in addition to his commercial work he is a volunteer photography teacher at the alternative school affiliated with Dolores Mission.

The following photographs are a selection from a book that the Venants are currently preparing of gang member portraits and interviews.

The room, draped with blue and yellow streamers, was dark and still. Save for a few muffled outbursts, no one would have known that it was packed with people.

Then a man ambled in, innocent-acting enough, his tin granny glasses and worn zippered sweatshirt lending him the air of a superannuated student.

Suddenly the lights flashed on. "Happy Birthday," the crowd brayed, as a glittering mariachi band swung lustily into the tune, accompanied by guitars and horns. Women rushed to embrace the man while beribboned children from the parochial school twirled among the crowd; homeless families gathered along the wall.

Then a line of solemn young Latinos threaded their way through the festivities. They wore sagging pants, long white socks, and T-shirts. One by one, they threw an arm around the man's shoulder, turned, and made their way to the rear of the room, where a banquet table was spread with sausages, beans, and coleslaw.

The gangs had come, not as gate-crashers, but as members of the community, taking their place alongside the children, the homeless, the women, the mariachi musicians. For a few hours, at least, they were simply teenagers eating hot dogs at a church party.

Surveying the gathering, the man, a priest, turned to a parish colleague: "This is the Kingdom of God," he said.

A small, rough stucco church, the Dolores Mission looks as if it should sit in the town square of a sleepy Mexican village. Instead, it is situated less auspiciously in East Los Angeles, hard by the cemented banks of the Los Angeles River. A five-minute drive from the office towers of downtown, just over a lanterned bridge that spans the railroad tracks, the church serves some 2,500 families who form the city's poorest Catholic parish and one of its most dangerous neighborhoods.

Taxi drivers routinely refuse fares to Pico-Aliso, as the district is known. When they do go, they dare not stop for traffic lights. Nine warring gangs claim territory in the public housing projects of Aliso Village and Pico Gardens; the walls are scarred with their signs, and the neighborhood is wracked by their violence.

From 1989 to 1990 the Hollenbeck Divison of the Los Angeles Police Department, which covers a major portion of East LA, saw a 30 percent jump in gang-related crime, compared to a 5 percent rise for the metropolis as a whole.

"I've buried a lot of kids in 1991," the Jesuit priest, Father Gregory J. Boyle, reflected the day after his thirty-seventh birthday. He recently officiated at his nineteenth funeral.

"That's all I need," he added with an edge of cynicism, "to become the burying priest of gang members."

Posted at the Dolores Mission five years ago, Father Boyle came to the barrio determined to reform the gangs. The young priest, the product of a comfortable middle-class family from the city's Westside, had been evangelized by the poor, working for a year with the Indians in the mountains of Bolivia. But when he walked in the streets of Pico-Aliso, the gang members would turn away, even "dis" (disrespect) him—staring him down, swearing in his face.

The priest countered, learning who they were and calling them by name. When they didn't come to his church, he went to them. Pedaling a bicycle through the projects, he visited the fractious gangs, listening to them. Eventually he received the ultimate honor: He was given a gang handle, "G-Dog," composed of the first letter of Gregory and a gang suffix.

Gradually the gang members began turning up at the church complex. They would "kick back" in a recreation room furnished with a sagging sofa and secondhand television set. They painted posters for church events and helped in the daily feeding of the homeless who came to eat and sleep at the church.

In 1988 the church opened an alternative school for gang youths across the street. Run by four Jesuits, it now has an enrollment of eighty-three and about half that number in actual attendance.

But in the past such accomplishments have been marred by community resistance.

An outspoken advocate of gang rehabilitation, Carmen Lima, admits that she used to have a negative image of the youths. Another community activist, beaming at Father Boyle's birthday celebration, says she used to want to run the gang members down with her car.

"People want to just discard them. But when you throw something away, it's going to be *somewhere*," says "Bebe" Breavon MacDuffy, president of the Pico Gardens residents association and one of the roughly 15 percent Blacks in the Latino neighborhood.

But over time the community has lined up behind the priests. Fueling their support has been a bitter conflict between the gangs and the police.

In September 1989, Captain Robert Medina took over command of the Hollenbeck Division. Then a 28-year veteran of the LAPD, Captain Medina was formerly a member of the Internal Affairs Department, responsible for investigating police misconduct.

Gang members, the priests, and certain neighborhood leaders had long charged Hollenbeck police with harassing the youths and taking them to nearby industrial depots, known as "the factories," to beat them up.

Captain Medina made his stance clear early on, telling

this journalist: "I just cannot believe that any of my people could be involved in that type of activity without me or my other captains or some of the decent law-abiding citizens in the community being aware of these things and bringing them to my attention." But decent citizens had been talking about police brutality for a long time.

One day Anita Moore, president of the Aliso Village residents committee, sat in a neighbor's kitchen sipping a glass of chilled fruit juice and talking about the LAPD and the local housing authority police.

"The kids were telling me about the police," she said. So when the housing police rounded up a group of four or five teenagers one day, she crossed the street to see what was going on.

"I was dumbfounded," she said. The police had the boys lined up against a wall and were hitting them with batons, she added.

"I just started crying. I couldn't believe it."

Moore shook her head. "The police say that all the kids want is to sell drugs. That's not true. They want a chance."

A group of gang members, gathered in the parish rec-reation room, also recalled clashes with the LAPD. A young man with a knit hat covering his forehead tells how police officers stopped him, a pal, and his pregnant girlfriend as they were getting into a car in an alley near his buddy's house.

"They pulled his girlfriend out. They started beating him down for nothing. They told her, 'Look at him.' After they beat us down, they let us go."

Last January, about the time LAPD officers were video-taped beating the Black motorist Rodney King, the mothers of Pico-Aliso, united in the Committee for Peace in the Barrio, called a meeting with Captain Medina and his men at the church to hear their complaints.

Says Father Boyle with a laugh, "The police had messed

with the wrong mothers."

Leaning on a rostrum before an overflow crowd, Captain Medina heard the full fury of their battle cry.

Defending himself, he said that he too was a poor boy from the wrong side of the tracks. He understood what it was like to grow up in the barrio. But their sons could also have a better life, if they tried; and he mentioned such symbols of success as Rolls–Royces and Jaguars.

But on the subject of police brutality he didn't budge. There was no proof that his men had used excessive force in dealing with gang members.

This was the position he had always stood by. "It arouses my competitive instinct, to put it mildly, when I have people making allegations without any substance to them," he had told this journalist a year earlier.

"For gang members," he said, "life means nothing. They have no respect for law and order, they have no respect for their parents, they have no respect for the rights of others, they have no respect for anything." The priests, he said, couldn't understand these things.

From his shoebox-size office at the school, Father Peter Neeley watches the gang members come to class. They swagger down the street like forty-year-olds. Their faces are hard and closed. A smile is a sign of vulnerability. A smile can kill you. Enemies crouch in the alleys, ready to pounce on the weak.

"The big thing here is image. You have to keep your image up," says Father Neeley, forty-four, a former sociology profesor at the University of San Francisco.

About three fourths of the school's student body of fourteen- to eighteen-year-olds are on parole, and the pressure to be *bad* is intense. "Don't go to school, don't participate," Father Neeley says. "The really cool guys are the ones who sit in the back of the class and make fun of the teacher."

School supplies that aren't nailed down often disappear. Fighting words are everyday forms of address.

"Their world is like that, so why isn't yours?" Father Neeley says.

But the Jesuits and their staff react to the subtext. They develop relationships that allow the gangs to let down their guard. "Nobody's going to make fun of you. Nobody's going to put you down," Father Neeley says.

One of the subjects offered at the alternative school is photography, which is taught by Pierre Venant, my husband. In these classes, "the darkroom has become a sort of confessional," he says.

Not long ago a tough-talking sixteen-year-old announced in the quiet darkness, "I was born in an egg." His mother is on drugs most of the time. Rejected, ashamed, he escapes the house, sometimes sleeping at the church.

The boxes of photographic paper are covered with graffiti, but the students handle the Nikons, cradle Pierre's Hasselblad, like crown jewels.

"You have to be very delicate," he told them one day, explaining how to focus with a telephoto lens.

"Yeh, man. It's like masturbating," a student replied with understanding.

Students now vie for darkroom time, sometimes printing into the evening, long after classes are out. They design photo assignments, describing the feelings of violence or beauty they want to express. They decide on locations—the wastelands surrounding the Los Angeles River, walls adorned with their gang's graffiti—and they make their pictures.

Creating images, they build a stronger image of themselves.

Still, persuaded to have their own pictures taken, they step onto the photographic backdrop of the no-seam paper, taped to a classroom wall. With all the machismo of hard-core thugs, they mad-dog the imaginary enemy, throw signs.*

Then suddenly one day the gang's glare cracks into a smile. They laugh, they clown for the camera, they call their buddies.

And they ask, "Hah, man, when are ya gonna take my picture again?"

---

* to mad-dog—to act belligerent; to throw signs—to make signs with one's hands that identify one's gang

TAX PAYERS
NITEMARE
TOUCHIN PAINT NITELY
GRAFFiTi KiLLR ALL *

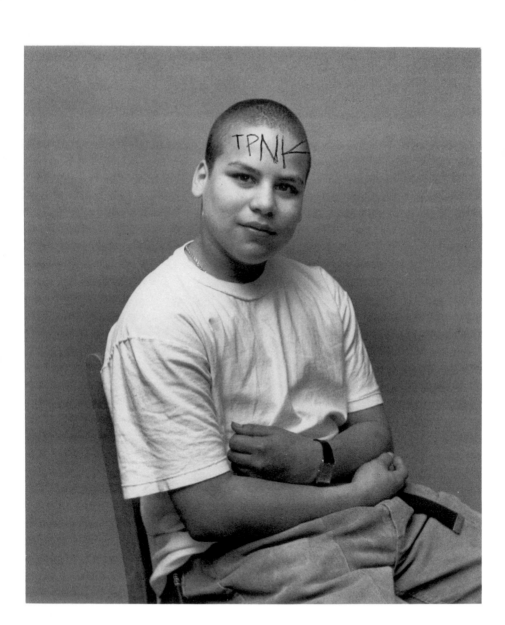

W/S PJC

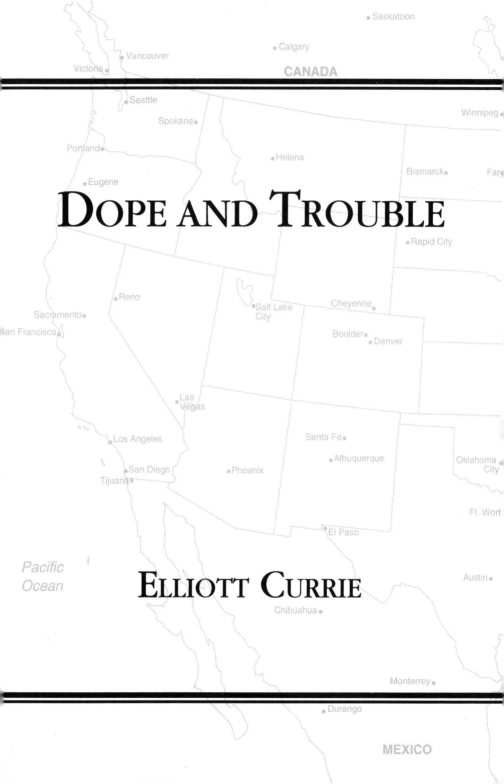

DOPE AND TROUBLE

ELLIOTT CURRIE

Elliott Currie was born in Macon, Georgia, in 1942. He is currently a Research Associate at the Institute for the Study of Social Change, and a lecturer in the Legal Studies Program, University of California, Berkeley. He is also Vice Chair of the Eisenhower Foundation in Washington, DC, which supports innovative delinquency and drug abuse prevention programs in the inner city.

In 1988 he received the first Donald R. Cressey Award from the National Council on Crime and Delinquency and in 1990, the Paul Tappan Award of the Western Society of Criminology and an award for Dedicated Service in the Field of Prison Research from the Prisoners' Rights Union.

Mr. Currie is the author of *Confronting Crime: An American Challenge* and coauthor of *America's Problems: Social Issues and Public Policy*. The following selection is an excerpt from his forthcoming book, *Dope and Trouble: Portraits of Delinquent Youth* which will be published in January 1992 by Pantheon Books.

Mr. Currie lives in Berkeley with his wife, Rachael, and daughter, Susannah.

T he two young people whose interviews follow are drawn from a group of several dozen I interviewed in the late 1980s in a public juvenile facility that I will call "the Hall." I went to the Hall in the first place to learn something about why growing numbers of young people were appearing in the child welfare, juvenile justice, and mental health systems across the country—at a time generally considered to be one of prosperity. Both the local and national economies were still enjoying what was often described as the longest economic expansion since the 1960s. Yet in the county served by the Hall—I'll call it River County—as throughout the United States, a wave of young people were washing into the public and private agencies of control and confinement. It was widely agreed among River County's social service professionals and juvenile authorities that they were coming at younger ages and with deeper and more stubborn problems—problems that were overwhelming the system's ability to cope. I wanted to understand why.

There was also a more personal, visceral reason. These kids, and the vastly larger army of "discarded" children and youth in the United States, have been for the most part conveniently hidden from view and denied the chance to be heard respectfully and seriously. We are familiar with the media image of the flamboyant drug dealer and the inner-city gang leader—but we know little of what they think or how they interpret their own lives and the world around them. And we know next to nothing about the kids who are more typical of the mass of American youth who move in and out of the juvenile justice and child welfare systems—the runaways and the abused, the car thieves and vandals, the ones who have gone over the edge on drugs or alcohol.

The Latin American writer Eduardo Galeano has said that literature should "make audible the voice of the voiceless," and that description fits these young men and women like a glove. They are, to begin with, very young, which in our society already undercuts their claim to have something important to say; worse, they are also officially delinquent, which compounds their "voicelessness." For those who are not just young and delinquent, but young, delinquent, and poor, the chance for a hearing is even slimmer; and for those who are young, delinquent, poor, and female, the deprivation of "voice" is almost total. I wanted to give them voice in part because I felt they had a right to be heard, and in part because I believed that depriving them of a voice is not only unjust but also self-defeating; when we block their capacity to speak and be heard, we insure that they will find other, more destructive or self-destructive ways of getting their point across.

It is terribly important, for our sake as well as theirs, to pay attention to what they have to say. For it is only when you have heard their stories that you can really comprehend the depth and meaning of the disaster that has afflicted youth and families in the United States in their lifetimes. We do now talk a great deal about the crisis of children and families, and we have even begun, haltingly and with only intermittent success, to promote legislation to do something about it. But I am convinced that most Americans simply do not yet understand how bad things have become for the kinds of people whose lives are described here (I know I didn't). These stories portray lives that are precarious and threatening beyond most people's experience or imagination. And as long as we keep those lives hidden, we will continue to fail these young people, and we will continue to jeopardize their futures—and ours.

Loca

She could be a rock star, or an actress. She's part Latino, part Anglo, vibrant and animated, with great masses of dark hair and an easy smile. A tattoo on her upper arm reads "Loca"; a smaller one, between thumb and forefinger, identifies her as a hard-core member of one of the most visible youth gangs in River County. She turned herself in to the Cherry Grove police to face charges of drug sales and assault.

At the end of eighth grade I became into this gang war kind of stuff. I was into this group that was called BGS, Barrio Grove Sur? And I loved the way they were, because they were always *laughing*, they were always get up and go, you know? And it was just something I thought I wanted. But it turned out I didn't, but I really *thought* it was what I wanted. 'Cause, you know, we would start fights all the time, or get *into* fights, and I'd always get my drugs free; they always had it. You know, they would sell it, but the money wasn't really an object to them, it was more as we were like a *family* together. Nobody would trespass against us, nobody would mess with us, nobody would touch anything of us, nobody would disrespect us or anything; it was just like, you know, we were just all close together and just have a good time. And that was our own little world.

And as it progressed I was lying a lot more, running away from home, and going on so-called missions, going from each little city, and meeting people and partying with them, in barrios. So it started progressing like that, and then when I became in like the middle of my high school years, about tenth grade, I dropped out of high school. I really wasn't *going* to school though. You know. I would go to school, but I wouldn't go to class. [Laughs] I would go off campus, I would go there to meet my friends and we'd go off campus and we'd just party, anyplace that we could go, we'd go party.

That was my daily routine. Getting up, not even getting out of bed, smoking a joint. Making the guy that I lived with, that we lived together, making him breakfast. Smoking joints all through that morning. Waiting for my friend to come over, we started drinking 40-o's of Olde English.* And then we would smoke a lot *more* joints! [Laughs] Visit some schools, you know, sell some joints. Go pick up a carload of friends. Go cruise around for awhile, but while all this, drinking Tequila, José Cuervo. And just drinking Olde English and smoking a lot of joints and KJ, that's the four main things really, that I would do.

KJ? that's PCP. When I heard it I thought it was coke and a joint! [Laughs] But then I found out it was PCP when I first smoked it 'cause it kind of tasted funny, didn't taste like coke and a joint. They just told me, call it KJ, so I did. KJ! What was the other word for it? *Fraho*, but that's kind of different. It was opium with PCP in it, or a *bomba*, [Smiles] it bombed your head, that's my definition for that.

Well, by nighttime we would be maintained, drunk, wired, stoned, everything you could possibly be. But by nighttime that means we're almost to the belligerent where, you know, nothing matters, somebody walks across your path, you're into a fight. Mostly every *night* we were into a fight. So that was mostly our daily routine . . . Then we'd sit down after a while and party some more and talk about, "Oh I could've done *this*, I could've done *that*," "Should've flipped him over like *this*," and "I should've stabbed him like *this*," and that was our daily

---

* 40-o—forty-ounce can

routine. But it was always fun because . . . [Hesitates, smiles] I like violence. That's my problem. I don't know why. I guess because it's a habit. A habit of getting into fights . . . [Trails off] I don't know why.

Did you get scared doing this?

Getting into fights? Yes. But . . . some of my friends, they were involved into a martial arts called chi? Have you heard of that? Kind of a brain muscle, or whatever you call it? But they kind of taught me how to control my mind. [Softly] And I would turn over my scaredness and sadness and every kind of feeling that I had, I would turn it over to anger. And that's how I got my name, Loca. I would get really crazy [Laughs] and after a while they tattooed me. See, Loca. [She is pointing to the tattoos along her arm] And I've got these, see, and I've got this, for [my barrio] . . . but soon as I get my act together I'm gonna have them taken off. I was gonna burn them off but that's too painful.

That's one thing I can't stand, the sight of my *own* blood. I don't mind anybody else's unless it's really really *gory*, but . . . [Laughs]

I've been stabbed here, and I've been stabbed *here*, and broke a *lot* of bones. I've broken my ribs twice, from chains mostly, getting dragged by a chain, like in gang wars? And broken arms, I don't know *how* many times I broke my arms, missing and hitting a car! [Laughs] Those kind of things. My leg's been broken a lot. I've had my head cut open back here. That was from a car accident. Well, I wasn't *in* a car, I just kind of got run over. I don't know how I survived out there, I really don't.

That's why people liked me, I was smart . . . I mean I knew a lot of things, what to do, you know. Especially like stealing. I would plan things out instead of just going in there and getting it. You know? I was a planner.

Then I started getting into a lot of fights. And then we started getting into a lot of gang wars, from different barrios to barrios, and getting into a lot of PCP and KJ and acid and 'shrooms and peyote and so forth. I did pretty much anything besides shoot up. I'm really scared of needles.

That's one thing, I love to travel. I'd say I've been to most of the cities around here. I love traveling. I mean going to each city finding out new things, about partying, new ways how to smoke pot, new ways how to snort *this* . . . [Laughs] It was a trip, I mean it was fun. Those were missions. Out of the blue, "Let's go on a mission, let's go on a mission!" And on our missions we'd go and we'd stay out for maybe three weeks just traveling . . . One night we'd be in Hillview, one night we'd be in Valley City . . . Valley City was a hip place. Winston Boulevard? It would take four hours to get down one side of the street, that's how *booming* it was. All it was, was just Mexicans from all different barrios would get together, you know, just cruise around, stop and party with *this* gang, stop and party with *that* gang . . . That's the way it was, it was cruising the boulevard.

And then when I started getting into that, I really liked it more, because . . . [Hesitates] you know . . . I felt in *control*, that nobody wanted to mess with me, 'cause, you know, I'm *bad*. You know: I can beat you up, I'm *down* enough to beat you up, I'm down enough to go into that store and steal a case of Olde English. You know? And so, I don't know, I felt really good about myself then. But I really didn't. [Laughs] But I thought I did.

They would call me the heart of the club, you know, the heart of the group, because I was bold enough to do anything that sounded illegal, or sounded a threat to society. And you know, that's what I *wanted*.

How come?

I was mad at the world because . . . [Scratches her head] I don't *know* why! But I was mad. I haven't found that out yet. I'm working on that. [Laughs] I don't know who I was mad at, I was mad at myself.

Your parents?

I was pretty much mad at them, too, because, you know, they weren't there when I needed them and I didn't know how to express to them that I needed help. The only way I did that was disrespectful . . . and it didn't really work, until later on in the years.

I don't remember too much of my childhood, you know, when I was really little. But I do remember I started stealing and lying when I was about in the second grade. And then we moved on to Arizona, 'cause my dad was traveling a lot so we had to move to Arizona. And there I did pretty okay, you know, not lying and stealing, all that. And we only stayed there for six months, and then we moved again out here.

And by that time I was in third grade. Stealing. Stealing became my priority then. I was stealing *little* things, you know, like candy and money from my parents to go get candy. And I was always lying. That's when I think I started my whole life, right there, down the drain.

And it was in my elementary years that I first started the taste of beer and alcohol. I think I was in fourth grade when I started drinking alcohol. And I liked it 'cause I'd see my parents drink sometimes when they were at home together. They'd drink a couple of wines and stuff, and I don't know, I was "How come *I* can't drink that?" So I was a curious little kid. And by the time I was in sixth grade I started smoking pot. Actually it was *fifth* grade. And I was stealing jewelry by that time, jewelry and candy, little knickknack things.

Sixth grade, that's when it *started*. [Laughs]

First time, I stole my mom's car and drove around. While in the meantime I was stealing a lot of alcohol from my parents, bringing it to school, sharing it with my friends. And at that time my sister—she's older than me, she's 21—and me and her kind of were really close together in our childhood, but then I kind of got jealous of her 'cause she had a lot of friends that were always *laughing*, and I wondered—Why are they always laughing? She was really a partyer. And I found these little pills in her room one day. And I thought they were candy! You know, I mean I never thought a little thing like that could get you all wooooo! [Laughs] So I just tried that, and I liked that. Because I just sat in my room for a long period of time, when my mom worked nights and my dad was out of town, and just *laughed*, you know, all by myself! And I thought that was funny! so I laughed some more! [Laughs] And so I started stealing those from her and she started to notice that they were gone, you know, missing some of them. And, you know, I denied it.

But then by the time I was in seventh grade I had my own connections of weed, and then I started getting into crack and coke, and like quaaludes and reds and . . . [Laughs] and on and on and on!

But then in seventh grade I started a fire in my school. Just for a laugh, you know. I don't know, in between my sixth grade and my seventh grade I was gaining a lot of weight. And that depressed me, but I also started getting real conscious of myself in between that time. And my mom was going to school, my dad was always out of town, so there wasn't really anybody there for me to talk to. And when my mom was finished with school, you know, I just kind of felt like well, I don't know how to talk to her, so I just would leave it alone. So I was getting more heavy into drugs. And a lot more like violence and stuff, you know.

Like when I was in seventh grade I hit up the walls, you know? I started hanging out with Mexicans. And after I started the fire I started forging checks. We had a candy run at our school and I used to forge checks so I could win a hundred dollars. I had big plans, yeah! [Laughs]

And that went on for a couple of years.

And I was running away between all this. I remember one time that I came home, I don't know *how* I got home though, but I remember how I was about ten miles away from my home and I'd been out for about a week or so and I was on a lot of drugs all at the same time. And I remember walking toward my house, but I don't remember how I got there. And I remember going to the door and *sitting* there for a minute and then finally ringing the doorbell. And I said, "Mom, take me to the hospital, I think I'm gonna die." And so she hospitalized me for that night and then she took me to a rehab. And I stayed there for a week, and I ran. [Laughs] After the drugs flushed out of me and I started detoxing. I was pretty much detoxing pretty bad. And so I ran with another friend that I made in there, or I should call acquaintance, rather than a friend. And I ran and I stayed out there for a week and I used all the same drugs and came back thinking I was gonna die *again*. And I was having a real bad trip and everything.

So I came back to the rehab, I finished off that program. I thought I was being honest back then but I really wasn't and it was just a whole game, that whole rehab was a game to me. You know, I could beat the system, which I did. I graduated from there, I stayed sober for about two weeks! Then I kind of kept it undercover for about three months. I'd go out, say I'm going to an AA meeting or something, and I would not go. I would go out, meet my friends and go party.

When I was living at home I'd get up every morning, smoke pot out of my window and I'd get ready for school and I'd go to school.

I went to Truman High School. That was the main drug school in Cherry Grove. You could get any kind of drugs there. And I would go there and I would buy about an eighth a day, and that was just for the school time. And I'd go to school, me and my friends, smoke pot. And I'd go to this one class which was my so-called favorite teacher, because he would do coke, you know, in the classroom. He was really a cocaine fiend. There's a lot of teachers there that drink in the classrooms too. It's a really bad school. [Laughs] Don't ever send your kid there, if you have any.

The teacher was snorting coke in the classroom?

Yeah, he did a lot of cocaine in there. And I found that out after I was his TA.* 'Cause I would start off good, you know, and I wouldn't do any drugs and everything, and I would go to school for about two weeks. And be teacher's pet. But then I became *his* teacher's pet, but he would always talk about partying. So one day I looked in his drawer, you know, to get some files out to correct some papers. And I seen a mirror. And a *razor* in there. I mean, what are you going to do with a mirror and a *razor*? [Laughs] You know?

So I just kept it to myself for awhile. And one day I came to school, I mean *really* out of it. I walked in there and I remember him just sitting there and closing the drawer really fast. And I said, aha! And I walked up to him, and I sat down, and I said, "You wanta smoke a joint?" And I just boldly handed it out to him. And then I kind of caught myself and I said, "I'm just kidding, it's just a cigarette." And he goes, "No, it's not, I can smell it on you every day." I said, "You can? How come you didn't say anything?" But a lot of the teachers there aren't really the kind

---

* TA—teacher's assistant

of people to tell on you, because we wouldn't have a population of the school, you know? [Laughs] 'Cause I only know two kids, really, that went to that school who didn't smoke pot.

It's really not a good school. Not at all. I mean I thought it was the *best* school when I went there, 'cause I mean, God! "You sell this, you sell this? Wait! I never *heard* of this!" [Much laughter] You know? It was really a trip.

When I got to that school I was just doubly shocked. I said "Whoa! All these *drugs!*" But I loved it. And then I met a lot more Mexicans there. That's when I got into that heavy violence thing. But most of the time during school I would stay at home, drink 40-o's. But when I'd visit school, on the way back, because I lived by the [train] station? We had to cross through the parking lot to get to the school. So we'd go to school, on the way back, stop by, pick up a couple Kenwoods, you know, stereos out of cars.

But I think I did learn a lot. Mostly math, I liked math. I was always wired in there, 'cause, you know, he gave it to me free! So it was like, I would do the work, I was always the first one to do my math. And I would always say, "Math is so *easy*." But what I really did was I picked out the easy stuff, you know, but actually I knew a lot of harder stuff than I really did. But I did learn a lot, like algebra and calculus, sometimes, and study those things when I went to class . . . [Quietly] and felt good about myself, I mean really good about myself, had a natural high, and I wanted to learn something that day, and I would study it, so I did learn. But I think people can learn from school *if* they want to. You can go to class, do the work, "Aw, this ain't teaching me anything," you know, but later on when you realize you still want to learn, that stuff will still be in your mind. I mean I still remember calculus . . . [Laughs] I'm surprised, I mean, from all these *drugs* . . . [Shakes her head] I *miss* school.

But after a while it kind of got worse, and I noticed it progressed a lot and I started doing a *lot* more KJ, PCP, and more acid and drinking a lot more alcohol, and then came the Mexicans again! [Laughs] And I was back to the same old thing, except that progressed too. The gang wars that we were having then were involved with knives and guns and chains and stuff like that, and that went on for maybe a year.

And, you know, driving crazy on the street. That's what scares me. [Shudders] I can't *stand* cars anymore, 'cause I remember the last time that I was *completely* out of it, but I knew what was happening, and we're driving down the freeway with no *lights* on in the opposite direction in the middle of the night! And *that* scared me. Yeah, I still have dreams about that, and I think that's keeping me not going out there. And I didn't get in a car again unless we were not partying. So I was kind of being precautious, but I was still doing the same things. Besides just getting into cars, because that scared me.

But I was still, you know, shooting off guns and getting into a lot of fights. And I'd been to jail a couple of times. Me and a couple of friends went to L.A. for a gang war out there and got caught. We had a fake ID because we would go to bars all the time. We had a fake ID on us, they'd bring us in, being over age we went to jail, and got to know people in there and became so-called hard core, you know. And I really *liked* that, you know? Because like, being in *jail* . . . [Grins] Hey, I'm *bad*, you know? I'm not even 18 yet! [Laughs]

And then I started getting my own apartments. And what I remember now, which I really didn't even notice, is I was paranoid of everything. I mean I *knew* it, but I wasn't really responding to it as though, why am I so paranoid? I would sleep in one position, you know, with a knife just like *this* crossed over me [Her arms across her chest], and I mean that's *crazy*! 'Cause I was selling drugs then, I was selling cocaine in large amount of quantities and I was selling a large amount of quantities of marijuana too, and I don't know, it was paranoia! [Laughs]

But I started stealing a lot more. I would steal about 300-400 dollars worth of clothes, or like we'd go on a run and we would steal a lot of jewelry from a lot of stores, and sometimes we'd steal from houses, which was progressing a lot. And then I kind of cut back on that and let other people do it.

I never got caught except in third grade. I almost got caught, though, in Cherry Grove Mall. OK, I was stealing a stereo, a disc player, out of Cherry Grove Mall. I didn't know that those wires, if you cut them, they had an alarm on them. Stupid me! [Laughs] They did! So I took it anyway, though! And it was me and another person I call my road dog, a good friend of mine, and another person I called her my little *granada*.* So we each had two bags filled with clothes and jewelry and all that stuff and we all had trenches on. So I had these wire cutters right here, and slipped 'em on this stereo and boom! [Laughs] Alarm went off! And I said "Oh no," and I already had the stereo, so might as well run, right? And we planned this out, though, of course! Me! and I had somebody waiting . . . at the *other* end of the mall! [Grins, laughing] All the way at the other end! And so it was pretty embarrassing because I seen a lot of my neighbors in there, from my parents' house . . .

Running down, like this, in a trench coat, all hard-cored out, with two bags, with a whole bunch of security men following me and my friend too, and my other friend too, I mean just *running* down the mall, "Move out of the wayyy!" [Laughs] I mean, I was jumping over little *kids* and stuff, it was crazy! But I never got caught. We jumped in the back of the truck, we all had this *bato* call, whistle,

* *granada*—grenade

you know [Whistles] and whistled really loud and luckily they heard us 'cause they started the engine, they were starting to go slow, we just threw the bags in, we jumped in, and that was it. Got away! But I thought I was really lucky then . . . I mean, that was a *lotta* clothes that we had.

One thing I do laugh about is, though, one of my other friends, her name is Shy Girl, she's really shy, but she had on pumps with a trench on so she lost one of her pumps, and that little thing . . . I always laugh at that.

It sounds like you guys took care of each other . . .

Yeah. It's always been like that. I mean like somebody would disrespect somebody in that barrio and I mean they were just *out*, I mean they were just gonna regret that for a *long* time. A lot of people went to *hos*pitals, you know . . . [A long pause] It really hasn't hit me too much though, right now . . . I don't know why but it hasn't. I mean there's a lot of people that I know that went to the hospital, you know, from *us* . . . [Hesitantly] I mean I could just imagine from *their* point of view, you know, "I didn't know they were so hard core and all that stuff, I didn't know they were crazy like that!" But I don't know, it really hasn't hit me yet, you know, the fact that I've broken *collarbones* and stuff, of people, just because they named something off at me, or something, like calling me a female dog or something? And me wrecking their *collar*bone . . . I can't believe that I even liked that . . . did that . . . today. I don't know *what* I am, how I'm gonna be, but I'm finding myself out.

The last time I went to jail was in Valley City and we had had a gang war out there. And I remember I went into the jail but I really didn't want to go that night, because there were a lot of 14s in there; I claim 13, the southside, and 14's northside. And there was a lot of 14s in there. And that means war! You know? [Laughs] So I really didn't want to go in there. But all I remember is I was really out of it, had just got done fighting, cops pulled me in, and boom, got in a fight as soon as I got in there. They took me out and put me in another cell and I stayed there for awhile, about two days, and then we had a gang war in *there*, 13s against 14s. Well, it got broken up, nobody really won, except a couple of people got stabbed.

Badly?

No, not really. I mean you can't really stab too many people, you know, unless in the eye with a toothbrush. [Laughs]

So that happened. And while I was in jail I really started thinking about my life. And I really didn't want this any more because that night, you know, too many guns were fired my way. And it started scaring me just like the car did. And I said to myself all right, when I get out of here I'm calling my parents and I'm gonna go turn myself in, 'cause I had a lot of warrants out on me. And I turned myself in and they were kind of shocked that I did because, you know, it was right before I turned 18. 'Cause I didn't want to go back to jail because I have enemies in there now too.

And so I did it unknowingly to my barrio, my gang, because if they knew that I was in here they would contact me and I know I wouldn't want to change. So I'm keeping that kind of cool.

But I'm gonna take my GED and I'm gonna go to college. And I'm gonna go in the restaurant business. I've always wanted to own my own restaurant. [Smiles] French! 'Cause I love to cook French food. And I've always wanted to be a chef too. I loved to cook, ever since I was a little kid. I'm surprised I kept that with me though. You know, being in the restaurant business. Ever since I was a little kid I've wanted to be a chef. Just kind of didn't work out that way. And that's pretty much my life story.

James L.

He's almost painfully slight, but his chiseled features and abundant dreadlocks make him look both vaguely regal and quite fierce. He has been sent to the Hall for a minor theft in Iron City, a charge he denies with convincing contempt. He thinks the real reason he's behind bars is his reputation as a leader in the recent youth gang wars in the city. It's rumored that, despite his youth, he is not only a major player in the local cocaine trade—having taken over a turf formerly held by his older brother, recently hospitalized with gunshot wounds—but a main gang "shooter" who has put several rivals in the hospital in his own right. The day after we spoke, in the worst gang violence in the city's recent history, a carload of youth from his neighborhood, Manorville, opened fire with shotguns and machine pistols on a group of young people from a rival turf, Bay Ridge, killing two and injuring several more.

He chooses his words carefully: guarded at first, he becomes increasingly warm and reflective as we talk.

My brother got shot up in Iron City, he got shot in the face with a twelve-gauge. He lost his eye, some teeth, and they was talking about it was all over a *gang* and all that. His name Leon? And they say he the Manorville gang leader, talking all that stuff, they trying to say he a gang leader, it was over a drug deal.

They been trying to say that my brother was a big-time gang leader and I was a *little* time gang leader, I'm taking over his drug business and all that type of stuff like this. [Scornfully] I'm in a *gang* and all this, I'm a big shot and all type of stuff like that.

But it wasn't nothing like that! It just like, you know, we all be hanging out together, we be hangin' in Manorville, cause one of my grandmothers stay in Manorville and one stay a few blocks away. So we all be hanging together like, and then these other dudes, we be going to parties and then they be talkin' all this, like, you know, "Y'all can't come over here," and all this. And we be like, "We just coming to the party," and we just start *fighting* and all that. And then they brought guns into it, and they start shooting and all that.

And like we was all out in Manorville one time and they was gonna come shoot us up like, you know, 'cause we was all out there having fun, there was about maybe forty or fifty of us out there, right? And my brother he seen them, so he chased them out of there, and when he was driving they started shooting at him and he was the only one that got hit. So like he really saved a few people lives, taking that twelve-gauge to the face.

He lived, though, he all right. He was in the hospital for about a month and a half or two, he was in critical condition for a week, they had to do all type of surgery and all, to get the things out. Then he stay in the hospital for a month and a half. So I was just like up in the city, running wild like, and then I just got caught up in some stuff and got busted.

It's gettin' kind of *dangerous* out there. 'Cause my mother just came up here and told me that one of my cousins he got shot, he *dead* now, his name Richard Sims? They had it all in the news and stuff, they saying *he* was the Manorville gang leader! [Laughs] See, they don't know, they just saying that he got shot over gangs and drugs and all this. But it was like he was just driving in the car with my other buddy, and the dudes, the same dudes that shot my brother, they shot *him*. Same dudes. And I know they ain't like—they ain't nobody, they just like, see, when they come to fighting they don't *fight*, they want to use guns and all that, you know what I'm saying?

But it seem like every time when somebody get shot over there from *they* side the police they be in Manorville trying to find out who did it and all this, investigating, but then when somebody from *our* side get shot they just like "Ha ha," *laugh!* They say, "Oh one of your guys got shot," then they *laughin'* and stuff.

With your relatives getting shot—do you feel scared out there on the street, with these guys coming around with guns?

Naw . . . not really. I don't be scared. They don't be coming through where *we* be at with guns. Only like—they might come through some time at night, or something. But I really don't even be *out* there at nighttime. It ain't like—you know, they just like—[He pauses] they like *us*, but they just . . . I guess they got they time to get us, like.

You know.

Every time, if it be gangs, they always say they fighting over *dope*. 'Cause one turf want to sell they dope over here and they ain't gone let 'em. [Earnestly] But that ain't what it be over! It's just over—like you know, you from Manorville, you from Bay Ridge, so they gone fight! *That's* what it's over! Like this been going on for years! I remember one time, it was about maybe a year ago, we used to be *hanging* with the Bay Ridge dudes! We used to go up there and be up there where they be, you know, chilling with them, hanging with them and stuff, having fun . . . you know? And then like, something happened.

One time they—like the *old* ones that's about 25 and stuff? They be like, "Yeah, a long time ago we didn't used to be like that, we used to be *fighting* them Manorville niggers," saying all *this* type of stuff, so that get the little young ones that's our age, they try to get, you know, all *tough*, thinking about it . . . So then that's how it got started, like. And then ever since then we ain't been cool with them, we just be cool with the Harrison district and Manorville, we just be together like. And then Bay Ridge, they just be with Richfield and a bunch of other turfs, and all that.

But that seems too bad, you know . . . here are these guys, and they're really just like you—young guys, living in the neighborhoods—but they're coming after you, and sometimes you're coming after them . . . Kind of sad, that you're shooting at each other—

Yeah . . . [Softly] It ain't no end to it though, I guess. I know they just gone be like that, since two people got shot already, it ain't gone be like . . . that easy. A few of *they* people up there got shot too. One dude lost his eye up there too. Another dude he got *paralyzed*, all *type* of stuff. I don't know.

 And then the police was trying to say, they was trying to get *me* on some of the shootings that happened up there, trying to say *I* did it, like I'm the main shooter. Like one time they jack me and they had the *news* cameras and all that out there, right, put me on the news saying that I'm known as one of the main shooters, the one most likely to be carrying a gun on me and, you know, telling who my *brother* was, and all this, and I go home and my grandmother she was *cryin'* and all type of stuff, she crying 'cause she's sitting right there and it was on the news, when I came in the house it was on the news. [He's looking at the floor] And, she was crying, and all type of stuff.

 Made me like—I put my hand on the Bible, told her I was gonna stay out of it and all that. Then I *was* stayin' out of it, wasn't gettin' in no trouble, just comin' in the house, doin' what she said, like. She was telling me like to quit being with my brother so much, 'cause he *older* than me, *much* older than me, he twenty. And she was saying, quit

71

being with him, just hang with my friends. And I was just hanging with my friends.

All it really is, it ain't over no drugs, it's just over who want to have the most *respect*, with the girls and all that, you know what I'm saying? That's what it's about, respect. They just want to be known the most to the girls, you know, to the boys that's just going to school and all that, you know? 'Cause like now the *girls* they ain't no good neither! [Laughs] They just want you, like, if you got money, or if you have a fresh car . . . Not *all* the girls but I'm just saying *most* of 'em is like that, they want you 'cause you got a fresh car or you got money, or you *known*, like everybody *know* you. So they just want to be, you know, known as your girlfriend, like. That's all it really is.

The girls don't be in this game, they don't be in none of this gang stuff. They just watch. They just watch so they can gossip, and tell who won and what happened, and you know. That's all they do.

(He moved into an apartment with his brother, until the brother was arrested for selling cocaine: "My brother don't have his apartment no more. Police took it. He going to jail for a while, for about five years maybe. One of his friends set him up, planted some stuff on him and snitched on him to the police. But this dude, he was supposed to be getting about ten years, and then he got out in two weeks! And he ain't been coming around no more. [Laughs] I was telling my brother, 'cause the dude seemed kind of funny to me anyway, I didn't ever trust him, like. But my brother, like that was his best friend, and you can't tell him nothin'. Like he going, 'Nun-unh, he cool,' 'cause he did so much stuff for my brother, know what I'm saying?")

I'm not saying your brother was into this, but you know a lot of people who're out there dealing drugs—why are they into that if there's such a danger of being set up, of going to prison?

Most people need the money, they can't get no job, most of 'em like messed up, cuttin' school and all that, and all that, you can't get no job. If you *do* get a job, you gone have to *wait* a while, then what you gone do [Laughs], you *broke*, ain't got no money . . . Then when you *do* get a job you ain't gettin' paid that much, you might get a job at McDonald's or something like that, $4.65 a hour, and that ain't nothin'! When people be out there making thousands! In just one day! You know most people just take the fast money, they just want they fast money so they can like, you know, help they *mother* out, or maybe buy they mother something . . . [Softly] Some people mothers on drugs . . . so they can't, like, they ain't got nothing else to do . . . Some of 'em ain't got no in*tel*ligence, so they don't know, they just do it to make their money.

I hear that a lot, about guys helping their mothers out, with the rent and everything—

Yeah . . . 'Cause most of the mothers be on drugs! And if you got little brothers and sisters, then, you know, you don't want to see them all *dirty* and all that, you gonna make money any way you could, even if you *do* have to go to jail. [Quietly] At least they'll have some money or something. And they don't be starvin' or nothin'.

'Cause I be out there seein' a *lot* of little kids, they all *dirty* and stuff, don't be dressin' all right and stuff? I know when I was out there I used to take a lot of little kids to the store, buy 'em little stuff, and I didn't even *know* 'em, like. Like all the little kids used to know *me*, calling my *name* and stuff when I walked past, talking to me and stuff, little kids like about four or five! [Laughs, shakes his head] You know, I'd just be giving 'em money and stuff, "Here, go buy you something to eat!" You know, just like—coming through, taking care of little kids, like. 'Cause I know I wouldn't want *my* little kids to be like that.

There's a lot of little kids like that where you live?

They's a *lot* of 'em. I remember on Christmas I was going out there giving little kids money, 'cause like on Christmas, you know, I used to see little kids playing with all they toys and remote controls, and little girls carrying dolls, and all type of stuff? And like when I went out there I was just looking around, me and some of my buddies, seeing how many kids, you know, *got* stuff, like. And like hardly none of the little kids *had* nothing. And I'm like— you know, me and my friends, *we* got *everything!* It's like we was taking they parents' money and stuff, we taking *they* money! So that's why I just—like, give the little kids money, 'cause you know, if it wasn't for me and my friends taking they *parents'* money, they would *have* something. Not saying they parents ain't gone go to some- body *else* and get it, but I used to just, you know, be feelin' kinda *bad* like, 'cause I'm having a good Christmas, but what about the little kids?

When I was little I had *all* good Christmases, all *my* Christmases was good. And I'm just thinking like, man, they don't *have* nothin'! I got all they money, *he* got all they money, so . . . All my friends, we havin' fresh clothes and all like this, while *they* ain't got nothing for Christmas. I was just like givin' the little kids five, ten dollars. Tellin' my buddies, "Give the little boy some money," and stuff, you know? Like little kids they'll come up, they'll ax you, they'll see you counting your money or something, "Could I get a dollar, could I get two dollars?" You know, *little* kids like! They shouldn't even really *know* nothing about money! [Laughs]

(He dropped out of school a few months ago.)

I'm 'spose to be in 11th, next year 'spose to be my last year of school. But I was just cuttin', wasn't going to school. 'Cause I *was* getting good grades in class and all of that. In math I got all the way up to algebra one, I passed that. Then when I got to algebra two it was like gettin' kind of difficult . . . Then I was just like cutting class, "Forget it, I ain't gonna go," 'cause it wasn't nothing but like *Chinamens*, Chinese in this class! You know, they all smart, they all *smart* in math, I'm feeling like, "Man! I don't know *what's* going on!" [Laughs] So then I'm just like, "Forget it, I ain't gone go to this class." I was just cuttin' and stuff.

Did you ask the teacher to help you out when you didn't know what was going on?

I was axing 'em *some*times. But, you know, I didn't want to ax every time . . . You be axing questions and everybody *looking* at you like, all in your *face* and stuff . . . The teachers be helping, they helped.

I know when I get out I'm planning on graduating from regular school, high school. When I get out I'm just gone move up to Rivertown with my mother, cause it's *slow* out there. I don't hurt nobody. And then just finish school, and all of that. I want to just go to college, and then go to cooking school and become a chef. That's what I want to be. A chef.

'Cause when I was little—I been like cooking ever since I was about nine or ten. My mother used to give us all a chance, like, to cook dinner, like me and my brothers? She'll be right there, and you know, just have us cook up a meal like steak and potatoes, vegetables and everything, you know, garlic bread, all type of stuff, just watch us cook. [Smiles] And then she's going, "You should be a chef when you get older!" 'Cause I was the youngest *one* and I used be cooking the best! You know, they be burning they stuff up and all that [Laughs], and I used to be cooking the best. And ever since then I just wanted to be a chef. Like I be cooking my own meals, sometimes. Not that my mother don't do it for me, but I just like, you know, "Lemme cook my stuff," and just watch her, and she show me how to do it, you know, how to put the right amount of seasoning in there and all that? She just showed me that.

It sounds like you got along real well with your mom . . .

I got along with her for awhile. And then she got on the drugs. And then I just stopped talking to her, just started living with my grandmother. My grandmother's like, she's been my—I been calling my grandmother "momma" and calling my mother "mom," calling her momma ever since I was little. You know, I just look at them like *they* my mother and father. 'Cause I really never had no father, like. I lived with my father for like maybe four years. Five years, something like that. That was when I was from a baby till I was about in kindergarten. Then after that, I just started to see him—'cause he was a merchant seaman—off and on I'd see him, you know. He'd pop up maybe three times, four times a year, something like that, sometime I'd go stay with him, he had a little apartment, I'd stay with him for the weekend. But then after that, I ain't seen him for *awhile*, like.

That must've been hard, when your mom started on the drugs. . .

At first it was like we was a real, like . . . regular family. Like we used to go to the movies, and do all *type* of stuff. And then when she first started off, one of her friends that she grew up with, she was on drugs like real bad. And then I guess somehow she just got my mother to try it.

And like on Friday night—my mother worked through the week, she wouldn't do no drugs all through the week or nothing like that. But when Friday night come, they started drinking, and then they'd start doin' they drugs. [Softly] And I could tell . . . when she was doin' 'em, like...you know, she *changed*, like, 'cause I *knew* her, you know? I just could tell when she was doing 'em. And then my brothers and them, they was tellin' me—I'm like the littlest one, and I wouldn't believe 'em, right, and I just be *cryin'*, and then I'd go tell her what they were sayin' and all that. And then *they* would get mad at me 'cause she be mad at *them*, right? [Laughs]—then they wouldn't be talking to me, so I was like, "Damn!" Then I just be callin' my grandmother and talking to her. And then just go and stay at my grandmother's for awhile.

She just like—at first she used to buy us like about eight pair of pants, like for school? You know, when you first go to school? She'd get us like eight pair of pants, eight shirts, you know, about three pair of shoes apiece, stuff like that, and then, you know, it just started getting *lower*, like. She'd get us like maybe five pair of pants, one for each day of the week. Sometime maybe four, and then she'd just like get us a pair of shoes, and it just started going *down*, like.

And so my older brother started making his *own* money, and he was sellin' weed, to make his own money. And she used to take his weed and stuff, 'cause she didn't want him sellin' it. So she'd find it, she'd take his weed, take his money. But then he moved with my grandmother. Then he was living with her, then *he* got in the fast life, and then *he* got on drugs. [Sighs] And then my other brother, the one that's in jail now, it was just me and him.

And then *he* start goin' to Juvenile . . .

I remember we used to come up here and visit him, I was only about twelve. I was going, "Man, I'm not *never* coming here." And then I remember when he was at the Farm, and we used to be going up there, visiting him and stuff, and he used to be out there working in the fields with all them *cows* and stuff? And I used to be thinking like, "Man, I'm following right in his footsteps." Then I went to the City [Juvenile Hall], was up there for about thirty-five days, just like he was, and then I came down here, I been here for a month, maybe I be here for two months, and *he* was here for awhile. But then I'm thinking, now he going to the penitentiary . . . [Shakes his head] I just want to change before I follow that step and end up going to the penitentiary. 'Cause that's the next thing, you know, I don't want to do that . . . I'm just trying to change, like . . .

Do you want to have kids of your own when you get older?

I want to get married. I want to have kids. I think I'm gonna have a kid by the time I'm 18! [Grins] That's two more years, I think I might have a kid by *that* time! But I know when I have my kid I'm not gone be . . .you know. . . like my father, I'm gone be a *real* father to my kid. You know. I want my kids to have a real father and real mother, like. And grow *up* right. You know? And they really could *be* somebody, you know, make good money and stuff. [He's quiet for a minute, looks at his hands.]

'Cause it just seem like most of the Blacks is just goin' down the drain. They killin' off each *other*, like. They put the drugs in they own—in the ghettos, like. That's where most of the drugs be. In the ghettos. And they give 'em them little welfare checks and *know* they gonna spend it on drugs, so the White man gettin' the money right back anyway! They makin' the money right *back*, the big man, whoever that is, they gettin' the money back anyway. So they don't really care. Like they should have more little job [training] centers in the ghettos or something, you know, *helping* people. You know, helping people get jobs and all type of stuff like that, so they can take care of they *kids*, and all this.

I just heard Jesse Jackson talking about this—about respect— saying Black people ought to stop turning on each other . . .

Yeah . . . [Slowly] I just be thinking, like Martin Luther King went through all this to get Black people equal rights and all that, and now we fightin' each *other*, just killing off each other. I just be knowin' he turning over in his grave thinking about all this! How he did all that, gave up his life, he wasn't using no violence or none of that, he gave up his life so we could like really get equal rights, you know, be treated the same. Now *we* fightin' each other, killing each other off . . . That's stupid! But you tell somebody that . . . [Pauses] They don't think like that. They just thinking what they gone do tomorrow or next week, and all that. That they don't think about is they gone *live* tomorrow, is they still gone be *alive* tomorrow, they don't think about nothing like that. You know, people just gotta stop and think! They movin' too *fast*, like!

But I know when I get out a lot of my friends will say I changed, maybe be saying I'm a *square* now, and all this. But it's just that I ain't gone be doin' the things I was doing at first. And I just, like, had time to think about it.

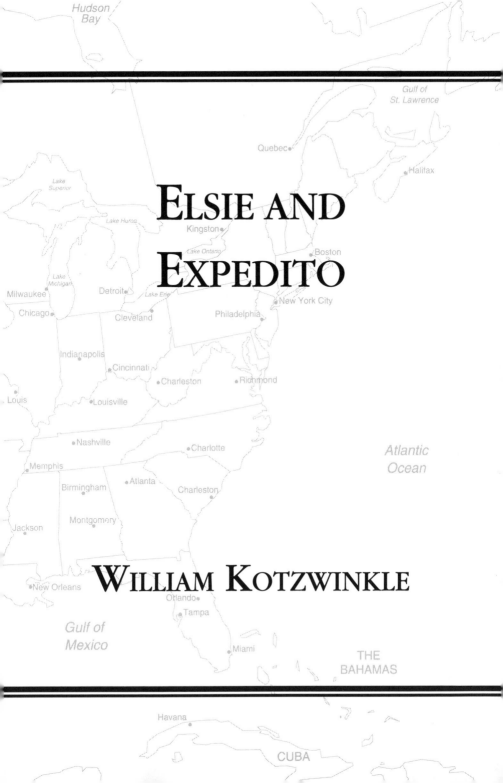

ELSIE AND EXPEDITO

WILLIAM KOTZWINKLE

Geoffrey Gammon Photography

Wwilliam Kotzwinkle was born in Scranton, Pennsylvania. He launched his literary career at the age of eight when he wrote a love poem for the character Wendy in *Peter Pan*.

Since that time, he has written a number of books, including *The Fan Man, Doctor Rat*, and *Fata Morgana*. His novelization of *E.T. The Extra-Terrestrial* was a best seller in 1982. His most recent novel is *The Midnight Examiner*. He has written sixteen books for children and is an accomplished poet.

Mr. Kotzwinkle's stories have been collected in *Prize Stories: The O. Henry Award, Redbook's Famous Fiction*, and *Great Esquire Fiction*. He has twice received the National Magazine Award for Fiction and has been nominated for the National Book Critics Circle Award. He now lives in Maine with his wife, Elizabeth Gundy.

The following selection is from his forthcoming collection of short stories, *Manhattan*, which will be published by Houghton Mifflin/Seymour Lawrence Books in Winter 1993.

Expedito stood in front of Tony Roma's Place For Ribs on 48th and Seventh, watching the crowds stream past. The smell of the cooking ribs filled the street, and he'd been salivating for about an hour. Dangling from the end off his arm was a tape player that played when it felt like; he gave it a shake but nothing come out of it, maybe later.

He headed east, tape player in hand. When food was scarce, the tape player got heavy. Today it felt like a black hole at the end of his arm, sucking away his strength, but he couldn't let go, it was all he had left from his old life as an orange juice squeezer and steady income.

The tape player kicked in as he stepped down off the curb. Music accompanied him across the street, toward Pizza Hut, salsa sounds carrying his tired feet to the front door. He stood there, tape deck playing, and breathed in the smell of warm bread and cheese. A delivery guy in a round white hat leaned against his van, eating a slice with pepperoni. This is the way of the world, Expedito. Today he eats, in his round white hat.

He walked east on 48th. In front of Manny's Musical Instruments guys were unloading amps from a UPS truck. The boxes were small, you could pick one up and go with it, but no, too many people around, you get yourself nailed, Expedito, and you hear the amplified sound of a cell door closing clang.

He crossed the street toward the waterfall, a stone wall with water running down it. He stood in front of it, rocking up and down gently to help his falling arches and breathing in the smell of water. He closed his eyes, and the water told him there were other lands, with jungle streams, where someday maybe he'd be, in a whole different life, pick an orange right off the tree. He opened his eyes and turned toward the entrance in the waterfall, a circular passage leading to a vest-pocket part.

The roof of the passage was glass and the water cascaded around it. He tipped his head back and watched the foaming water rushing around him. It was lit from within, pale green, pale white, streaming down on two curving walls either side of him. I could be in a barrel going over a waterfall. They find me below, bobbing to the surface. Crowd of prominent people on the shore, come to watch. A big shot step from their midst, says a man that brave deserves a break, says he ought to manage an orange juice stand.

He walked through the passage into the little park. One wall was hung with potted plants drooping down. Their tangling vines shone bright green. He walked along in front of them, fingertips touching their leaves and coming off filthy with soot.

Kind of job I should have, dusting leaves, In your commercial establishment or your public park. Little pail of water and a rag, and then make the rounds. Plants got to breathe through their leaves. It's a known fact you talk to a plant it grow better. You dust it, same thing. Everywhere I go, plants get a thrill, here come Expedito with his dust rag.

He let the charming dream go, let it slide off him with all the others that slid off him as he wandered.

He walked through the park slowly, past a Hindu guy on a bench, suspicious of me, like I'm going to rob him. Hey, I'm just here to dust the plants.

He sat down on an empty bench by the circular fountain in the courtyard. Water, Expedito. Agua. You tell me what it is. Does anybody know? No, they don't know. Nobody know.

Wandering the streets had led him to deep speculation like this. When you don't eat, you dream, and when you don't dream, you speculate. He'd speculated all over town. On buildings, on clouds, on bugs, on whatever he saw while he sat, hungry. He'd been squeezed out of his orange juice job and tossed on the street. I go the employment agency, tell them I'm a skilled orange juice squeezer, they tell me stick around. I wait all day, nobody calls in for an orange juice squeezer and I leave, sore from sitting on their metal folding chair. Shifting, shifting, all day on a folding chair. It break you down, and you don't go back. You walk around town, ruining your arches.

Two men in business suits were walking through the park, one of them poking the air with his finger, as if sticking it into somebody's eye, and said, "I understand him all right. I understand him five hundred percent." He continued poking his finger as they walked under the waterfall.

Water. Nobody know. They pipe it in here, but they don't know.

His tape deck clicked on, the music blending with the water's bubbling sound. He turned up the volume a little and the tape deck cut out. He banged it on the edge of the bench but no go.

A middle-aged couple came through the park, the husband short, fat, the wife tall, skinny. The wife said, "The last time I saw someone who looked like you he was dead."

"All right, all right." The husband glanced at the plants. "All right, I'll do it."

"I know what you'll do. What you always do." She was looking in the window of the shop that opened onto the park, and the husband was space traveling, off in a short, round rocket, lift him over the city.

Expedito turned back toward the fountain for some more speculating. How did the drops of water form? Did they feel anything? If I was a drop of water in the fountain I'd be going around and around all day. But I'm not a drop of water, I'm me. But I could be a drop of water.

A woman shuffled into the park, and stopped at The French Bakery Café, a rolling concession booth that sold crepes with a variety of stuffings. Expedito watched her choose, his stomach watching too. She paid and made her way to the other side of the fountain, where she plopped down on a bench.

Her clothes were peculiar, and her hair was wild and knotted, but to the trained eye, reflected Expedito, we see this is a woman has a source of income and a room somewhere. One, she bought a crepe, and two, she hasn't got everything she own in a shopping bag.

He studied her with interest now. The potted plants over her head hang down similar to her own crazy hairdo. She's talking to her crepe also, this is an important point, she's nuts how much we don't know.

As an orange juice squeezer, working at the same counter every day, he'd never known how many crazy people were paddling around, but he knew now. He was headed that way himself, because being on the street pushes you toward the place where your mind is weak. You can't believe you're really on the street, it seems like a dream. And pretty soon everything's a dream. And then you're crazy. He could feel craziness waiting for him, he knew what it would be like, he'd had hints, had found himself talking to inanimate objects from time to time. And they'd seemed interested.

The woman looked up suddenly from her crepe, and her eyes met his through the fine spray of the fountain. She moved her lips, as if speaking to him, but the bubbling of the fountain drowned her out.

He sat where he was, not wanting to scare her by any sudden movement. If he scared her, it she felt threatened and moved away, he'd never connect. So I play it cool, is all, and let her go on eating.

He watched as she ate and smiled when she glanced his way again. His clothes weren't too bad, only a little shading here and there on his jeans and denim shirt; if you didn't look too close Expedito Corales could be an orange juice squeezer on his lunch hour, you don't need to be afraid of him, lady.

Now she's done eating, now you get up and amble over slowly, that's it, casual approach. And turn back toward the fountain. Your jeans fit good, nothing torn on them, only a faint musk deep in the fabric come out with a single washing. And now, turn toward her. This is not a dream, Expedito, this is action with consequences; this will not fall behind you lightly as a dream. And what comes down, comes down, because I'm out here starving.

"How're you doing today?" he asked, in his voice of a working orange juice man.

She noticed he had a faint orange light around him. She frequently saw lights around people, it was part of her unfortunate condition. Sometimes they disappeared inside their light. Then they looked like lamp shades and she'd have to wait until they came back. This was part of her unfortunate condition too, for which she took pills. "I just ate lunch," she said, trying to be sociable.

"Yeah, I saw." He sat down beside her in his orange light. "Good, was it?"

"Now I take a pill." With a jerking movement, she took out her pill case. She'd noticed that many of the people at the hospital moved that way, like they never figured out exactly how everything works. She used to know how everything worked, but not since her precipitating trauma. Her precipitating trauma had put knots in her joints.

"I eat here sometimes too," he said. "But usually I eat at the little park over on 45th, you ever eat there?"

She lowered her head and noticed that her clothes were on crooked, her belt twisted sideways, and her blouse buttoned wrong. She had dressed very carefully but it came out this way.

"Well, people eat where they eat, it don't matter," he said. "Long as they have enough, right?"

"I have enough."

"Sure you do, you had a nice crepe, what kind of stuffing if I might ask?"

"I don't remember."

"Well, main thing is you ate it. It's in there, doing you some good." He had to step lightly, not press anything too much. Win her confidence, Expedito, and you will wind up going through her wallet to help her make purchases. Physical violence shouldn't be necessary, but we get in a hallway alone or some similar opportune situation, survival of the fittest is going to come into play.

She felt a dark wave come sideways at her from him, break over her, and flow away. The doctor said these waves were her paranoia, and she took pills for that too. "I like dogs, do you?" she asked, as she was supposed to attempt social interaction when she felt her dark waves, and she'd been developing an interest in dogs lately, which her sister said was a compulsive fixation.

"Sure, I like a dog."

"They eat too much. That's what my sister said. So I can't have one."

"What's your sister got to do with it? You live with her or something?"

"She drops in to see I'm okay."

So that's it, thought Expedito, the sister keeps her from going off the deep end. "And your sister don't like dogs."

"She's got a dog. It's okay for her, but not for me. Because I'm disabled, she says. Do I look disabled to you?" She straightened with a push of one hand on her spine and the other hand pushing up on her ribs. "Look at my posture."

"Better than mine," he said. "I have round shoulders from when I'm a kid."

"She ought to let me have a dog. For company. She's

got a husband for company, I've got hallucinations."

"You could have a small dog don't eat much."

"Tell my sister. She helps me sign my disability papers."

"What, you get like compensation, so much a month?"

"I can't sign papers, big deal. So she comes and helps me sign. I have to rely on her."

"Sure, I see."

"You like dogs?"

"Definitely."

"You have a dog?"

"That's a funny thing, I mean it's funny you should ask, because I been thinking of getting a dog myself." Expedito, a scenario is developing here. Don't push hard, just touch lightly. "We could, what do you think of this idea, we could go to the pet store and look at dogs. Maybe help each other out."

She turned her gaze toward the fountain and stared at her lifeless reflection, which was her catatonic posturing said the doctor. A strand of hair fell down around her cheek and hung there. Her sister said it was unsightly when her hair hung down like that. She pushed it back now because the orange gentleman was interested in her. Hoping to further conversation, she asked, "What about a cat?"

"In some ways better, you don't have to walk a cat."

"But they have no personality."

"Depend on the cat."

"I used to have lots of personality. I used to be able to make the sun come in and out."

"Yeah, that's personality all right." Expedito ran a finger lightly along the buttons of his tape deck, making sure it was off. He didn't want it to come on sudden and scare her away. Because we're making progress here, her purse is on my side of the bench, and the Hindu guy is leaving the park. I could just grab and run.

"That was when I was in the hospital. I was responsible for every death in the world then." She continued gazing at her reflection. "Or I could get a bird for a pet." She turned toward him. "What do you think of that idea?"

Expedito noted that her eyes didn't seem to focus on you, they focused like somewhere behind you. He looked toward the crepe seller, that was the problem, he could be trouble if he was the hero type. No, I got to get her out of this park.

"Or a goldfish," she said.

"You don't get much action out of a goldfish." He was tense, he was hurrying it too much, but she made him nervous. She was a fruitcake and he was worried about becoming a fruitcake himself. A solid month of squeezing oranges would straighten him out, but now he was in a fragile condition. He felt her weird thoughts could influence him, which was already a crazy idea. Just grab her purse, Expedito.

No, no, relax. Let the situation develop. "You don't mind my saying, a bird don't give much action either."

"You don't like birds?"

He nodded toward the pigeons that were pecking around the park. "Out here, okay. But a bird in a cage?"

The water on the fountain became suddenly still and she saw her own face clearly. My eyebrows should be plucked. And it looks like I put my makeup on with a spoon.

"That's a beautiful ring," said the orange man, pointing to her ruby. "My mother had a ring like that." He reached over and touched the ruby with his finger. "Do you think you could take it off so I could see it more closer?"

"I can't get it off. My fingers are swollen from the medicine I take."

"Maybe with soap."

"Do you have any?"

"Not on me, no."

She spread her fingers out so the orange man could admire the ring. Maybe he'll move in with me. If he can give me enough courage to buy a dog, I'll ask him if he wants to move in. The doctor said I shouldn't be so isolated from the world.

"Yeah," he continued, "just like that, my mother had. I used to love to look at it. It made me feel better, looking at her lovely fingers." Expedito had been raised by an uncle whose fingers had usually been balled in a fist hit him up the side of the head, but now as he told of a mother and her ring, he believed it, like all his other dreams that would slowly drive him as crazy as this lady fruitcake. "It's truly beautiful. Truly. And how I wish my mother were still living."

"I'd like a dog who'd treat me with respect."

"You train a dog, he'll respect you."

"You train dogs?"

"You hit him with a rolled-up newspaper."

She thought to herself: He knows how to train a dog. He'd be valuable around the apartment for that reason, and he could also make sure I don't burn the place down like I almost did when I was in a catatonic posture and melted the tea kettle on the stove. "I'd have a dog, I'd hit him with a newspaper and he'd respect me. We'd get along fine."

"Tell you what, I got a little time before my lunch hour end, let's walk over to the pet store. They got one on Seventh Avenue not far from here." He stood, his tape deck in his hand.

She squinted up at him. He was already taking charge. This is what I need. A nice orange man to sign my compensation papers and turn off the stove. We'll watch TV together and I won't tell him I cause all the news in the world. We'll be happy. "And we'll buy a dog?"

"We'll buy a dog."

"What kind?"

"Any kind you want. But—" He pointed toward the street. "—it depend on how much money you got to spend."

She stood and walked with him across the park to the street. He'd got her pepped up. He was good for her. She was acting in a social manner. She'd sociably ask him to move in with her, and they'd sit in the kitchen chatting.

"Maybe you should check," he said, "see you have enough money for a dog."

She watched the little crocodile crawl out of his head. It opened its jaws and its sharp white teeth glistened, the tips covered with blood. She'd have to ignore it if she was going to overcome her paranoid posture and have healthy social interaction with this man.

When we get to the pet shop, thought Expedito, I move fast. She got enough to buy a dog, she probably just cashed the disability check. Could have a couple hundred on her. Minimum twenty-five. She bring out the money, and I grab it. Stop looking at me, lady, that look is totally bananas, if it's contagious they take me away in a net.

She followed the little crocodile's progress along his forehead. Then it crawled back into his head, the tail twitching nervously back and forth and finally disappearing. "Well, that's an improvement."

"Yeah, you had some kind of spell it looked like."

"I'm troubled by anxious expectations. It's ruined my social life."

Anxious expectations, Expedito. You have a few of those yourself. Tell her about all the anxious expectations you've got.

"My sister isn't going to like this." Thinking of her sister made her knees lock, and she felt herself walking like a wooden soldier. "Helen says I have the discrimination of a four-year-old. But she doesn't know everything. I used to be independent. I used to work selling tokens in the subway."

There'd be some traffic jams with her making change, thought Expedito. Unless she's one of those crazies do complicated figures in their head, tell you how much anything adds up to and they can't lace their own shoes. "What stop you work at?"

"Fiftieth Street IRT. Right up the block. I liked it in that little booth. It was cozy." She looked toward the subway entrance on the corner with longing in her eyes. "But I experienced some criminal violence and became unbalanced."

And you're going to lay some more criminal violence on her, Expedito. Okay, I keep the violence to a minimum. A punch in the head, no more, if that.

"I was held up at gun point. Some kids dragged me out of the booth and tossed me around. It was at that point I became unbalanced." She felt her voice getting wooden, as she repeated the medical report. "I became paranoid and defensive. I was unable to trust. I experienced severe reality loss." She walked along with mechanically wooden strides, in rhythm to the sing-song of her voice. "And so Helen had to take over. Now she runs my life."

"Hey, you get a check every month from the government. You earned it, it's yours. Helen don't have anything to do with it."

"She fills out the papers. Will we have to fill out papers to get a dog?"

"No, they give you papers already filled out. Tell you where your dog come from."

"I don't care where he comes from. I just don't want to have to deal with papers." She stopped suddenly, feeling threatened. "I'm not dealing with any papers. Papers are worse than crocodiles."

"We'll buy a dog don't have no papers. He'll be cheaper that way."

"Fine, that's the dog for me." Relief flooded her. This guy had all the answers when it came to dogs.

"They got expensive dogs, and they got cheap ones. What kind you want?"

"I want one to sleep at the foot of my bed."

"A little one. Maybe a Chihuahua."

"No, they look like rats."

He reached for her purse, caught a flash of cop uniform out of the corner of his eye, adjusted accordingly. "Well, you could make it a cocker spaniel."

"You take your tape recorder on your lunch hour?" She nodded at the deck.

"Yeah, I like music."

"Let's hear some."

He pressed the play button, nothing happened. "Broken."

"Maybe the batteries are dead." She tapped her head. "My batteries were dead. But they recharged them."

She's a fruitcake, thought Expedito. I ordinarily would not steal from a fruitcake but I'm starving, and she'll get another check next month.

A wave of hunger hit him. He could smell roast beef, mashed potatoes, gravy. With a meal like that in him, he could think straight. And it's all in her purse, I'm so hungry I could eat the leather straps.

He was weak and dizzy, with a black mood creeping over him. He wanted to grab the purse and run before he hit bottom; he looked around desperately, but it was too crowded and there was a blue uniform in the crowd. You panic, you do something rash, you get nailed, Expedito, my son.

They turned onto Seventh Avenue. The weight of his tape deck was pulling him down. She was walking along stiff, and his hunger was mounting. Beat her over the head, knock her in a doorway. Eat.

His legs were giving out, he needed to sit, but she was propelling herself like a penguin. His tape deck kicked on, and salsa came out. It was the sound he'd been carrying for months, the song of his wandering, his soundtrack. When he got this hungry, the song could make him cry.

"This song have a lot of emotion," he said.

"My dog will be there in the night when I wake up."

They were headed down Seventh, toward the pet shop he hoped he remembered right. When you walk hungry your mind shifts things around. She scratched her head violently as if after fleas; he saw she had scabs on her scalp, patches of blood from digging with her fingers.

"Helen was always the queen bee. Screw Helen. Helen, screw you. This is from me. Yours truly, your sister. Signed in duplicate. And returned."

This is what today has brought you, Expedito. Make the most of it. Don't blow it just because your arms and legs are weak. Pull strength from the center, punch her in the face, and go.

"Step in this doorway, I got an idea. About a dog."

"There's the pet shop! You got me to the pet shop."

"Count your money. Here. Count it here." His tape player was still playing. He pressed stop so he could think what to do, but he couldn't think, he felt confusion. She was leading him, he went along.

"We can't look in the window," she said. "Or I won't go in. I know me. If I look in the window, I'll be intimidated. And I'll walk away, experiencing spasms and severe reality loss."

Severe pocketbook loss is what she's going to be experiencing, Expedito. Why are you hesitating?

"Fine, we go straight through," he said, head spinning. He wasn't used to burning energy like this, he conserved all day, but she was hurrying stiff-legged along and he hurried with her, the tape deck like a horse weight on the end of his arm.

"What's your name?" he asked, dragging beside her. "I should know your name before we go in. It looks better."

"Elsie."

"Slow down, Elsie. You're going too fast."

She turned at the doorway of the store and went through; he followed, into the smell of animals, birds, a heavy cloud. It hit him, he swayed dizzily, and a lady clerk came toward them suspiciously.

"Can I help you?"

"Yeah, this is my friend, Elsie. She's looking for a puppy. I came along to help her. We'll just look around."

"What kind of puppy would you like?"

"Moderately priced." He looked at the line of cages, then said to Elsie, "See one you like?"

"I can't get a puppy. Helen will kill me."

"Helen don't own you. You want a puppy, you get it."

"They've all had their shots, they're fine healthy young dogs, and you can take one home today," said the clerk, pushing for a sale, dogs must not be moving.

"I want one to respect me," said Elsie. "I've got the newspaper."

"Well, we have miniature poodles. They're very intelligent." The clerk pointed to a puppy leaping up and down in its cage and yapping madly. Elsie stared in at it.

"Not your dog," said Expedito. "Nervous dog like that will have a bad effect on you." He wanted to angle her down to the end of the cages, behind a stack of boxes piled there. The smells were weakening him, along with the heat, it was like a steaming jungle, and he wasn't used to heated rooms. The parrots were screeching and chewing crazily at the wire on their cages. He was trembling in the knees, the strength running out of him, and the wild sounds of the birds further confusing him.

Elsie turned to the clerk. "Helen doesn't want me to have a dog." She turned back to the cages and moved slowly along them, peering in at each animal. She'd made a crucial step toward independence by coming in here, her doctor would be proud of her, and she and the orange man would take a puppy home. But would the orange man want to live with her? Would he leave his independent life? I'd make him breakfast every morning and supper every night. I'm no prize but neither is he, he's got a crocodile in his head. I'm so tired of being alone, I'd give anything to have a companion. But what would he want with a disturbed woman like you, Elsie? He might like me buying his food and cooking for him, and all he'll have to do is check the stove now and then when I fall into a catatonic posture. Is that asking so much? And I'll wash his clothes, they need a washing. And buy him a new pair of shoes, his are worn out.

Tear the pocketbook off her, Expedito, rip it straps and all, and down the block, you can make it.

"We have some fine Dobermans if protection is a consideration."

"I don't need protection," said Elsie. "I control the news."

"I see."

He stepped between them. "Why don't you leave us discuss it? My friend don't have much experience in this subject."

He watched the clerk back away, because people will back off if you express yourself. His gaze fell on a package of dog biscuits that said *Chewy Flavor*. He started salivating.

"Look at this one," said Elsie, pointing to a round brown and white hound. She put her finger to the cage and the puppy licked it. A warm sensation ran through her, from her fingertip to her toes. "Did you see that?"

"Yeah, it seems to like you." He tore himself away from the dog biscuits. Now, Expedito, grab her bag now, and crash out of this place. Surprise is your ally. Shock and surprise. Like a panther through the jungle. Dogs and birds will cover your exit.

"Here, puppy, puppy." Elsie tried to get her hand through the wire of the cage, and the clerk came over.

"Please, don't."

"Don't what?"

"Don't put your hand through."

"My hand wouldn't fit through. I used to work in a cage. Hello, puppy, puppy. Are you my puppy?"

Expedito brushed away his fatigue, raised his head. "How much for this puppy?"

"It's a lovely little hound, almost pure beagle."

"Yeah, how much?"

"It's fifty dollars."

"Elsie, you have fifty dollars?"

"Sure. So long as I don't have to sign papers." She opened her purse, dug around in it. She stopped, looked up at him. "You sure I can handle a dog?"

"Anybody can handle a dog. You feed it, you walk it." His eyes were burning their way into the darkness of her bag. In there was his lunch and supper and a room for the night. In there was a repair job on his shoes, new sole and heels. He stared at it and saw everything he needed tumbling out like from the horn of plenty.

The puppy was yapping, excited by Elsie's attention. It knows, thought Expedito. It could be out of its cage today. Getting fed three times a day. Chewy flavor dog biscuits. "Give me your purse, Elsie." He looked up at the clerk. "She needs help counting her money."

There, Elsie, she said to herself, he's already proving himself helpful. But show him you're capable of functioning on an adult level, dig out your money all by yourself.

"Here you are, miss." She pulled out a fifty dollar bill and handed it to the clerk. "I'm buying that puppy without further notice."

"There's sales tax, of course."

Complications, she said to herself. But you can handle it, Elsie. "Here." She handed the clerk a twenty. Helen said I shouldn't be trusted with money, but Helen can go shit in her hat.

Expedito watched the money fly. The clerk was turning away, the purse was open, it'd be easy now, now is the moment to grab it. Action!

"Will I be able to give it a good home?" asked Elsie, turning toward the orange man and the words coming out of her like frightened, fluttering birds. "You know all about dogs. Will I have any trouble?"

"Feed it good, that's all." Now, Expedito, now!

The clerk lifted the puppy out of the cage and handed it to Elsie. She set her purse down on the counter beside the dog biscuits. The round little hound licked her twitching face. She felt tears coming to her eyes. I'm having a real emotion. I must be happy. "What a sweet puppy. And you're my puppy."

He grabbed the bag of dog biscuits and raced with them toward the door.

"Sir!" The clerk hurried after him, but he was out, underneath the tinkling bell of the door.

"It's okay," said Elsie, "I'll pay."

"Well," said the clerk, turning back toward her, "in that case—"

"He's independent," said Elsie. "It's an important quality." She watched the door through which the orange man had raced. "We were supposed to go home and sit in the kitchen with puppy."

"You'll want a collar and leash, of course."

"I was able to talk to him because he wasn't judgmental like Helen. We could have gotten along. But I don't blame him. I know I'm a difficult person."

She took the little hound's paw in her hand and shook it toward the street. "Puppy and I say goodbye."

Expedito hurried along the street, tearing open the bag of dog biscuits as he walked. He reached in, brought one out, bit into it. The taste of meat burst over his tongue. Chewy flavor. Filled with nutrition. Everything you need.

Clutching the bag tightly under his arm, he vanished into the crowd.

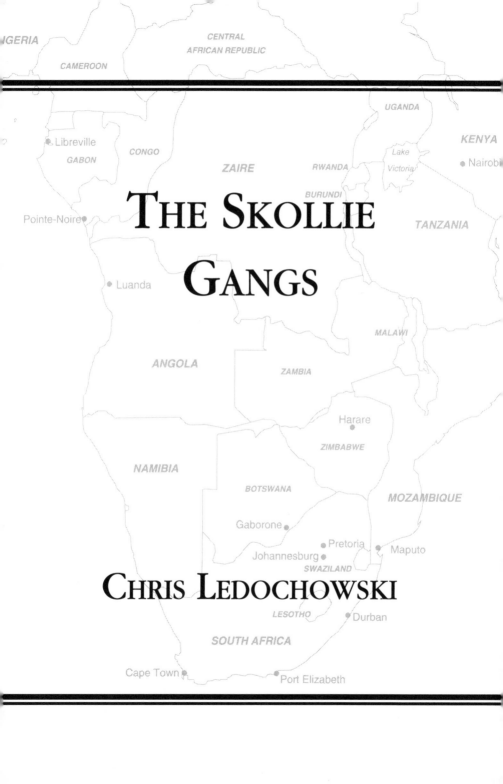

THE SKOLLIE GANGS

CHRIS LEDOCHOWSKI

Chris Ledochowski was born in Pretoria, South Africa, in 1956. He studied photography at Michaelis School of Fine Art in Cape Town and later joined the Afrapix Photographic Collective.

Mr. Ledochowski has done documentary work on squatter communities and on unions and progressive organizations in South Africa. He is now a member of Southlight Photographic Agency.

He has worked with gangs in a number of South African townships, taking individual and group portraits of and for the gangs, which he hand-tints and which he is not at liberty to publish. The following photographs are drawn from his work with the gangs and are published with their consent.

In the early 1960s the South African government began constructing the "Cape Colored" townships—Hannover Park, Manenberg, Bonteheuwel, Bishops Lavis, etc.—in what is known as the Cape Flats fifteen miles north of Cape Town. The townships were designed as temporary housing for people moving from the outlying rural areas to Cape Town in search of work, many of them attracted by the industrial expansion there. They were also built to accommodate those who were to be forcibly removed from Cape Town and its suburbs by the Group Areas Act.

One community within Cape Town that was to be evacuated, District Six, was an old, colorful, and vibrant section of the city in which people of various races coexisted peacefully despite apartheid legislation. The population was predominantly Black and working class, with a mix of Whites and Indians as well. Traditional cultural bonds between members of extended families were tight, providing a strong economic as well as social network. This translated into self-sufficiency for extended families, each having one or perhaps two breadwinners and sharing living quarters. District Six was a self-contained community, having everything from tailors to fishmongers. Few of its residents were dependent on the government or on factory work.

Like other racially integrated communities in South Africa, District Six was a thorn in the side of the designers of apartheid, a reminder that they had not been entirely successful in their efforts to categorize and separate the population on the basis of race.

In the late 1960s the South African government fully implemented the Group Areas Act. It required the forced relocation of the entire population of District Six, some

40,000 people, to substandard government housing projects, or "dormitory townships," in the desolate windblown region of the Cape Flats. Meanwhile, District Six was leveled.

The relocation had an insidious economic rationale as well. It was synchronous with rapid industrial expansion in the area around Cape Town, which in turn required a vast influx of workers.

In the Cape Flats dormitories, extended families were no longer able to share living quarters; instead, they were divided among one-family units. Each nuclear family now had to pay rent separately, which required that one and sometimes both parents seek employment. By breaking up extended families and rupturing their economic safety net, the government had artificially created a labor pool. The new township dwellers had little choice but to take one of the low-wage jobs in the new industrial centers ringing Cape Town. Previously self-sufficient communities like District Six became totally dependent on the factory wage system.

The abrupt uprooting and transplanting of District Six precipitated the deterioration of the economic, environmental, and social conditions of the community. With their concrete courtyards, the cinderblock apartments of the Cape Flats allow no privacy, and the sparse vegetation of the area makes for a deprived environment. Over time, inferior education, the slow unraveling of the extended family structure, and ultimately the disintegration of the nuclear family became standard features of the Cape Flats. The rich culture of Muslim and Christian traditions was sustained only in part and with difficulty. Moreover, as the economic circumstances in South Africa began to deteriorate, albeit gradually, unemployment became increasingly common.

With the collapse of community support and control structures and the cultural traditions that had sustained them, township youths created group identities by banding together in gangs. The gangs structured themselves along military lines, a practice that originated with prison gangs. However, these teenage *skollie**gangs differ from the earlier gangs of District Six in that they are a direct result of the apartheid system and the capitalism it embodies. The former District Six gangs either disintegrated or adapted to the new townships.

In South Africa you are a gangster if: you are unemployed and steal in order to feed your family; you are pressured into joining a gang; you join a gang to gain group protection; you are involved in the drug or liquor trade; or you have spent time in reform school or jail. There you will almost certainly have been forced to join a gang, and you will carry its identifying tattoo to the grave. Once you have a tattoo, it is unlikely that you will be allowed employment in mainstream society. More likely, you will be forced to continue operating in the informal sector—hawking, drug trafficking, and the like.

Gangsterism now literally rules the Cape Flat townships. For most residents, gangs are associated with senseless terror and violence. The bleak dormitory surroundings are decorated with the names of prison gangs, old gangs from District Six, and local gangs whose names and styles are often greatly influenced by personalities featured in the American media, particularly TV, as well as by movie idols and pop music stars. The gangs are a cold reality, an added strain on people already having to bear up under governmental repression and grim environs. A resident of Cape Flats who is not protected by a gang is often vulnerable.

It is important to see these developments in the larger context of the apartheid system. It has created a grave situation in which people's options have been heavily

---

* *skollie*—ruffian

circumscribed; under these conditions it is much more likely for someone to resort to illegal means of making a living. It does not help that gangs are frequently sensationalized by the media or portrayed as heroes. Gangsterism, often used as a convenient hook on which to hang the problems of a township, is a symptom of deeper social and economic problems.

The look of innocence is never to return to the face of this youth from Manenberg township.

Three group portraits of township youth, portraying the development from young playful groups to hardened gangsters. The last portrait features the lieutenants, captains, and generals of the Americans, the largest and most feared gang in Hannover Park township.

Taking photographs of gangs is not a simple affair, as most members do not want to be identified. Taking photos for gangsters—both portraits and group shots—is a rewarding experience, even though these photographs may not be published. These three photographs, taken in public places in the Cape Flats, were taken with the agreement of the groups.

The ever looming presence of gangsterism, Hannover Park township.

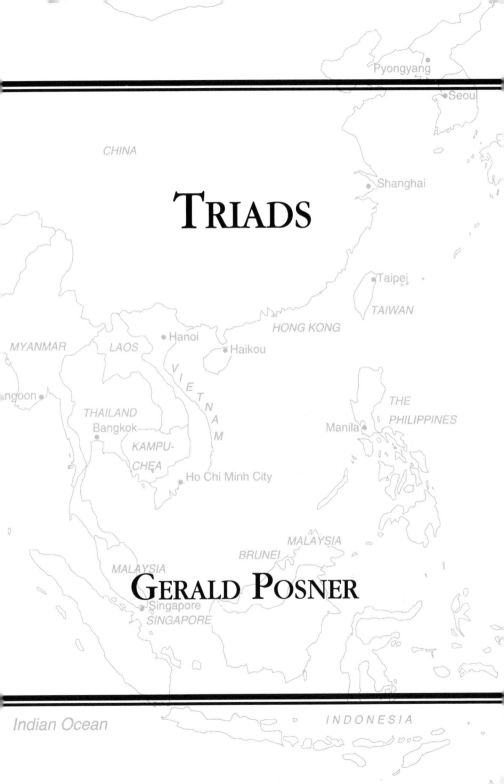

TRIADS

GERALD POSNER

Gerald Posner

Gerald L. Posner was born in San Francisco, California, in 1954. A writer and journalist, he received a law degree from the University of California, Hastings, where he was editor of the *Law Review*.

In 1986 he published his first book, *Mengele: The Complete Story*. Since then he has written three books, *Warlords of Crime—Chinese Secret Societies: The New Mafia*; *The Bio-Assassins*; and most recently, *Hitler's Children: Sons and Daughters of Leaders of the Third Reich Talk about Themselves and Their Fathers*. Mr. Posner's articles have appeared in the *New York Times*; *Chicago Tribune*; London *Observer*; *Himet*; *The Traveler*, and many other publications.

Mr. Posner lives in New York City with his wife, Trisha.

I had been through the narrow alleys and congested backstreets of New York's Chinatown dozens of times and enjoyed the exotic sights that draw tens of thousands of visitors annually. For me, Chinatown had always felt safe, its congestion giving a sense of security that crime would not strike. The restaurants offer plentiful food at cheap prices; the stores are filled with knickknacks and clothing at a fraction of uptown prices; and the 300,000-plus Chinese residents (officials can only guess at the number of illegal aliens jammed into five-story tenements) have converted a once Jewish and Italian neighborhood at the southern tip of Manhattan into a veritable slice of Hong Kong. It adds up to a tourist attraction that is hard to beat; even jaded New Yorkers find an afternoon or evening in Chinatown diverting and pleasurable. But my view of these streets changed one icy February afternoon in 1987 when I accompanied a retired New York City police officer on a walking tour. We began at Mott and Canal streets, a major intersection in the ever-expanding Asian community. It did not take long to realize that buildings I had barely noticed in the past held a very different meaning for someone in law enforcement.

"That pagoda-style building on the corner is headquarters for the On Leong," he told me. The On Leong is a tong, a merchants' benevolent association. Tongs are rumored to run some of the gangs that control extortion, gambling, prostitution, and drugs along those narrow streets.

We walked down Mott Street. Along the way we passed half a dozen stairways that sloped steeply down to unmarked door. I had always presumed they led to the basements of the street-level stores below which they sat.

My escort corrected me. "Most of those lead to men's

social clubs, and a few house the largest illegal gambling halls you'll find in this city. Try to get inside and see if you have any luck."

Even more surprising was the revelation that some of these basements were connected by underground tunnels to other buildings, sometimes as much as a block away.

"So if the police chase someone inside, he can just slip into the connecting tunnel and pop up in any of several locations, all far from where you think you trapped him," my escort told me.

In less than a block he pointed across the street to a small group of young men, all in their early teens, gathered in front of a store. Despite the blistering cold, they were lightly clothed in black denim jackets or thin dark overcoats. They all had thick black hair combed straight back in a pompadour and hanging long down their necks.

"There are some of the gang members," he said as we crossed the street to view them close up. "Their long hair is a sign of identification—they like being recognized down here. They only wear black and white, and I'll bet you they have on white T-shirts under those coats."

"What are they doing out here?"

"It's their territory. That might even be a gambling club behind them. But those kids aren't out for trouble. When they are looking for heat, they won't be standing still."

They were talking loudly in Chinese when we passed, one of them trying hard to look older as he took a slow drag on a cigarette.

On the next block my guide pointed out a liquor store. "It's owned by one of the prime movers in the Chinese underworld. I'm sure this fellow is tied into everything from dope to running girls. This is just one of his legitimate investments."

"Do the people in Chinatown know who owns this store?"

"Most do. There are no real secrets down here. Most

residents could walk you over to the Vietnamese gang hangout down on Canal, or take you around the corner and introduce you to the Hip Sing tong and their Flying Dragons gang. Hell, you just passed the Ghost Shadows gang headquarters up the street and you didn't even know it."

"But there's no sign of problems down here," I said.

He laughed. "That's the point. Everything looks just fine. It's only under the surface that you discover there is a real bad underbelly down here. There's heavy-duty racketeering and gang problems. It's just that the senior members of the community don't want to scare away the tourists, so they keep the problems under control." He shook his head. "Come on, I'll show you some more. Whatever you see today will only be worse in a couple of years. It's all changing with the gangs coming out of Hong Kong. Chinatown isn't going to be the same. It's going to be as bad as Hong Kong one day."

It was another month before I had the opportunity to see firsthand what this retired officer had meant. In sharp contrast to the chilly streets of New York, it was a balmy spring day in central Hong Kong when I followed a police escort into a narrow alley.

We stepped out of the sunlight through a portal and entered a dark maze of concrete tunnels. More than a hundred years of neglect had left the stucco walls blackened with dirt. Small doorways on either side led to connecting tunnels. The low ceiling was crisscrossed by a jumble of dusty wires, dangling electrical cables, and exposed fuses. It was difficult to walk on the uneven chunks of concrete that served as a crude floor. Occasional naked bulbs cast weak light, and the ceiling and walls closed in as we proceeded further. We soon had to bend over and walk single file. After several minutes the lead policeman's flashlight illuminated a crudely painted

115

wooden sign hanging over an opening to our right. "See that, it says the name of that street is 'Rat's Piss.' That's where we are going."

We turned into a tunnel choked with a mixture of hot air and strong odors: ammonia, freshly baked bread, burning plastic. From tiny rooms that opened up on each side, streaks of light shot into the middle of the pathway. In the rooms, men and women operated an assortment of antiquated equipment. In some, emaciated men molded sheets of metal over open pit fires. There were no windows. The heat was oppressive, making it difficult to breathe.

These were underground sweatshops. Standing in the tunnel, I understood why these workers have an average life expectancy of only forty-five years. They breathe in noxious chemicals banned by governments worldwide, are pried into inhuman working conditions, and are paid less than a dollar a day for work that kills them.

"That's why tourists can buy a shirt for $2 on the streets of Hong Kong," one of the police said. He went on to explain that while few people are aware of it, it is because thousands of people work in these conditions that the bargain center of Asia can flourish.

We were in the Walled City, an area only one hundred yards wide by two hundred yards in length. It was originally a military base constructed by the Sung dynasty in 1197 to manage the salt trade. With 50,000 people packed in its high-rise tenements, it is the globe's most densely populated patch of land. Rats and rabid dogs run in the alleys. Mounds of garbage rot in the dark stairwells and tunnels. There is little electricity, little running water, and no sewage system. Residents of the Walled City must climb as many as fifteen flights of stairs to reach one-room apartments that house two generations of the same family.

The tenements and tin shacks are crowded together and piled on top of one another, and all are connected by an intricate system of tunnels. It is possible to visit all of the

Walled City without ever seeing daylight. Children growing up within these confines seek a way out of their natural hell.

"This is Triad ground," I was told as we walked beyond Rat's Piss Street and further into the City. Triads are the largest criminal organizations in the British colony. The Hong Kong Police have estimated that each of the biggest Triads, like the 14K, have up to 30,000 members. There are at least fifty secret Triads in Hong Kong, with over 150,000 hard-core members.

The Triads' common symbol is an equilateral triangle symbolizing the three basic Chinese concepts of Heaven, Earth, and Man. The societies were founded in the late seventeenth century by Buddhist monks, not as criminal organizations but to achieve a nationalistic objective: to overthrow the Manchus, the "barbarian" Mongolian tribes that had seized control of China only thirty years earlier. Despite the Manchus' overwhelming military strength, strong pockets of resistance flourished. A key locus of anti-Manchu sentiment was a monastery in southern China where 128 militant Buddhist monks, who are said to have developed the form of self-defense called kung-fu, organized local resistance groups. In 1674 the Manchus sent a large force to attack the monastery. The assault was vicious, but the monks miraculously held out for more than three weeks. A traitor helped the Manchus gain access to the monastery through a secret entrance, and all but eighteen monks were killed. The Manchus relentlessly hunted down the survivors, finding and killing thirteen of them. The remaining five are credited with having established the first Triad society. Their avowed purpose was to oust the Manchus and restore the imperial Chinese dynasty.

The bloodletting at the monastery did not quell the resistance but served as a rallying point for anti-Manchu sentiment. More Triad cells were established. Despite

117

Manchu efforts to smash them, they continued to thrive. The Triads developed elaborate initiation rites and were bound together by an intricate system of secret rituals, oaths, passwords, and ceremonial intermingling of blood. As time passed, new recruits were given stringent physical tests, instructed in the history of the Triads, and sworn to blood oaths vowing allegiance to the society ahead of family or life.

During the 17th and 18th centuries the Manchu dynasty disenfranchised and alienated millions of Chinese and gradually chipped away at Chinese tradition. Hordes of citizens sought membership in the Triads, and hundreds of new secret societies were formed to accommodate them. Triads became the primary instrument for frustrated workers and peasants to express social and political grievances. Crimes increasingly were reported to the Triads instead of to the police. The societies operated as arbiters of guilt and innocence, and later as unofficial local governments. By the mid-1800s Triads were the recognized authority. They had usurped many of the Manchus' administrative roles.

In the mid-1800s some of the Triads made significant if abortive attempts at revolution, including the seventeen-year Taiping rebellion, the "Red Turban Uprisings," and the Boxer Rebellion. In response, the Manchus attempted to crush the Triads and nearly succeeded. In the face of these serious setbacks, the Triads' popular support diminished and their local income disappeared. Faced with extinction, the largest of the Triads resorted to an assortment of illegal activities including piracy, smuggling, and extortion. By the late 1800s the economic survival of most Triads was based on illegal revenues instead of the small contributions from local supporters. This was a critical transformation: The Triads metamorphosed from nationalist organizations into the criminal empires of today.

In 1911 the successful revolution resulted in the forma-
tion of a Chinese republic. There were an estimated 35
million Triad members, many of them highly placed. With
widespread influence in the new government, the secret
societies became increasingly corrupt. They degenerated
into vast criminal syndicates that rivaled the Sicilian Mafia
in size and organization. When Mao-tse Tung and his
Communist armies swept to power in 1949, the Triads fled
the mainland and flooded Hong Kong. There they formed
a new and dangerous extension of their criminal organizations—violent youth gangs. The Triads and their gangs
took control of the underworld in the British colony, and
today it still serves as their base of operations.

"This place is self-contained in almost every way," one of
the police escorts in the Walled City informed me. "It's
primitive, but they get along. They have food shops and
dentists and doctors and their own herbal pharmacies, and
they never need to go anywhere. And it's self-sufficient as
far as the gangs are concerned as well. There are gun shops
that make little shotgun pistols from scrap metal. If they
don't blow up when you use them, they can be handy.
There are hiding places for narcotics. There are gambling
houses, card halls, places to stash jewels after a robbery,
doctors who will fix you up if you get hurt and who know
how to keep their mouths shut. As a matter of fact, everyone in the Walled City knows how to keep their mouths
shut. They don't trust outsiders. Although some of them
work outside, they are loyal to where they come from."
 Not only is the Walled City a safe haven for the Triad
gangs, but its poor residents are also ideal victims. In the
absence of police authority, they are helpless against the
gangs. Sometimes a young girl is gang-raped, and it leaves
her so ashamed that she barely fights if her family is forced
to sell her to a gang, which in turn will sell her to the
porno trade or as a prostitute.

Young boys are also taken from their parents and sold by gangs to child pornography rings in Thailand and the Philippines. Stronger boys, some as young as eight, are enlisted to act as couriers for drugs and gambling and extortion payoffs. Others are intimidated into selling drugs at their schools. Typically, almost a hundred Hong Kong children between the ages of nine and fourteen are arrested each year as drug pushers. There are more than 5,000 registered addicts in Hong Kong who are under the age of fourteen.

Families in the Walled City are threatened unless they allow gangs to use their apartments as hiding places or for safe storage of illegal goods. The brave few who defy the gangs are made into public examples: Their mutilated carcasses are left in the tunnels, usually to be discovered by some returning schoolchild.

Two days after my shocking visit to the Walled City, the police introduced me to a former gang member turned informant, Benny. He was one of the very few truly fat Chinese I met. The cheeks of his Buddha-like face moved like jelly when he walked, and an engraved ivory toothpick dangled from his yellow teeth. He appeared ready for a Las Vegas gambling junket, dressed in a black silk shirt, bright blue silk blazer with extra large paisley designs embroidered on it, white socks, and black crocodile shoes. Benny had a criminal record of gang activities from the age of thirteen. He was now in his late twenties and managed a small jewelry store. He adamantly claimed that although some of his friends were still in the gangs, he was completely legitimate. Benny became my unofficial guide to the Hong Kong underworld.

A couple of days later, Benny took me to a nightclub where he promised I would see some of the young Triad recruits for the Hong Kong gangs.

There was a line of young people at the club when we

arrived. Benny forced his way through the crowd, and we entered a large room with deafening rock music, strobe lights, and a dance floor. Lounging around the bar surrounded by girls were young men in tight white jeans and T-shirts emphasizing their muscles.

"There are the kung-fu toughs," Benny screamed to me as we strolled past, to be sure I could hear him over the music. He stopped me. "Look at them for a moment. They may look pretty scrawny, but I want you to study them. Most of them, they grow up on the streets. In order to survive here you must be able to handle yourself—these guys know the martial arts from a young age. It's survival for many of them. These kids you see at the bar, their muscles may not look very big, but I tell you that if they are in a fight they are some of the toughest killers you ever see. They can be half destroyed but they continue to fight. They are taught from the earliest age that no matter how badly they are hurt in a fight, even if their arm and leg is broken, they must cause greater suffering and damage to their enemy. So if I think like one of these guys and somebody breaks one of my arms and one of my legs, I will think to myself that I will break both of his arms and both of his legs. Then I will win. When you have two people who fight like this—plus you must remember that it is part of our culture not to show pain or hurt—then you will understand how many street fights lead to death. Until somebody dies there can be no stopping."

The ability not to show pain or hurt is an interesting trait shared by these hoodlums. Benny explained that strength is honored in Chinese culture. In the gangs this unwillingness to allow others to see their suffering has become a badge of honor. Moreover, the Chinese are traditionally much concerned about "face" or standing in the community. Many Chinese will go out of their way to maintain face so that their honor and the honor of their family will not be sullied.

The refusal to suffer the smallest humiliation often creates a one-upmanship that makes the Triad members both reckless and dangerous.

"There are so many of them. I'm just surprised that they are all attracted to the criminal underworld," I remarked to Benny.

"Hell, you've got to remember they don't think of it as 'the criminal underworld.' For them, the Triads are just the best way to make a good living. They are fourteen or fifteen and they live in some half-condemned building with thousands of other families, and all they can dream about is owning one of those nice BMWs or Mercedeses they see all over Hong Kong. And they don't want to wait twenty years working like their father in the kitchen of a restaurant serving tourists. They want the money now, and the only way they can get that money fast is by joining a Triad. A kid can make ten times as much in one month collecting protection money from a nightclub like this as he can make in an entire year of breaking his back in a straight job. What do you think these kids will choose, especially when they see friends who have joined the Triads come back to the old neighborhood with a solid gold ring and a nice silk suit. They want the same things."

Benny later introduced me to a young Triad member, a rising star in the Hong Kong underworld. He epitomized what Benny had explained as the motivation for joining the Triads. He was impeccably dressed in elegant linen trousers with a silk shirt and an expensive silk blazer. His large gold Rolex watch advertised his monetary success. It was that visible material accomplishment that lured young teenagers suffering in Hong Kong's most impoverished environs to join the Triads.

During my time with Benny I discovered that Hong Kong's poorest neighborhoods, like the Walled City, serve as the Triads' recruiting base. The Hong Kong Police even acknowledge that Triads recruit at schools in poor areas.

Gangs often "rent" children to run an errand or pick up a package. As junior apprentices, these children admire older gang members, hoping one day to attain the swagger and wealth that is the trademark of the successful hoodlum.

There is no minumum age requirement for a potential Triad member. The younger the better, in that the Triad has a chance of indoctrinating him completely into a criminal life-style. The Triad bases its decision on whom to recruit not only on the poverty in the district but also on the recommendations of current members. Sometimes a Triad member may know an up-and-coming bully in a local school or some youngsters experimenting with drugs—these are people likely to move to the top of the Triad recruiting list.

The Triads also recruit adults, often in prison. It is considered fertile ground, since an inclination toward criminal activity is a prerequisite for full membership, and there are few places better to find such an inclination than among convicted felons. Some Triad members are usually in prison at any given time, where they continue to serve the organization by recruiting. The most violent prisoners often are given a telephone number to call upon their release. That outside contact helps arrange introductions to Triad members who will independently decide whether the prospective member is worthy of admission.

One of Benny's disclosure's that most surprised me was that membership in the Triad is very selective. "No one can join unless they are chosen," he said. The Triad's primary criterion is loyalty to the organization. The elaborate initiation rituals are intended to weed out those who might not be suited for membership. The secret Triad ceremony illustrates the unusual nature of the Hong Kong societies and the type of person who will answer such a rigorous call.

The traditional Triad initiation took several days, but

many Triads have shortened it to less than a day and dropped some of the more elaborate rituals. However, some items have remained constant. Each recruit has to be recommended by a current member; without such a sponsor one cannot attain membership. On the day of the ceremony, the new recruits learn the history of the Triads from a senior official dubbed the "incense master." They then kneel in front of several stuffed dummies, and while the incense master stresses the need for absolute loyalty to the Triad, another member chops the dummies apart with a sword. This shows the recruits what will happen to them if they betray the organization.

Then a Triad member presses the edge of a knife against the chest of each recruit, asking, "Which is stronger, the blade of the knife or your heart?" "My heart," the recruit answers, meaning that even the threat of death could not make him betray his Triad brothers. The incense master then reaches the main part of the ceremony, the reading of thirty-six oaths that were created in the earliest days of Triad societies. The oaths emphasize the undying loyalty of the new member to the society, and each initiate repeats the promises after the incense master. Nearing the end of the modern ceremony, a chicken is usually killed in front of the recruits. Its blood is mixed with blood taken from the punctured finger of each new member and then intermingled in a large cup. Each recruit drinks from the cup while being warned that if he betrays the Triad blood will be let out of five holes of his body, both eyes, both ears, and mouth.

At the ceremony's conclusion the new recruit often has to pay an initiation fee, the amount varying with the reputation of the Triad.

Benny thought the ceremony helped to keep the Triads exclusive, as opposed to gangs that anyone could join. That exclusivity, as well as the aura of invincibility surrounding the Triads, has fueled their success. The Hong

Kong Police admit that Triads are now more powerful than ever.

In 1997 the British crown colony of Hong Kong will revert to Communist Chinese control. Many of the largest Triads are afraid of a Communist crackdown and are looking for new bases of operation in Australia, Europe, and the United States. In New York, Triad advance teams have already arrived and established operations. In five years their operations have skyrocketed from running only three percent of the heroin trade to controlling almost eighty percent, displacing the traditional heroin brokers, the Sicilian Mafia.

Youth gangs affiliated with the Triads have become more brazen as they have grown in power. Restaurants and gambling clubs have been shot up by gangs in disputes over small pieces of Chinatown turf in U.S. cities, leaving dozens dead and wounded. In 1988 and 1989 the FBI and the Drug Enforcement Administration cracked Triad smuggling rings, each of which was responsible for bringing almost a ton of pure heroin into the U.S. Although each case set a new drug seizure record for U.S. law enforcement, the street price of heroin did not increase, as other Triads quickly filled the void and provided vast new supplies. In 1990 a funeral was held for a slain leader of the Vietnamese gang Born to Kill. At the graveside four young members of a rival Chinese gang, the Ghost Shadows, who were disguised as mourners, suddenly dropped their bouquets of flowers to reveal Uzi submachine guns and opened fire into the crowd. The two gangs were working for the same Triad in different sections of New York's Chinatown. The shooting at the funeral was motivated not by ethnic rivalries but by turf battles.

David W. is a 31-year-old waiter in San Francisco's Chinatown. He has lived in the neighborhood since his arrival from Hong Kong nearly thirteen years ago. He sees the gangs daily, and although he avoids them he is worried about the rampant crime they are generating within the Asian community.

"No one likes them here, but there is nothing we can do. If you go to the police, the gangs find out and punish your family. They really can't be touched. And they know it. So they just get worse all the time, and it's not good for any of us. They bother a lot of shops for money and everyone pays. It's just easier. No one wants trouble with them. There are more of them since the time I first came here. Definitely more. You don't have any idea."

But by studying the Triads it is possible to know what David is talking about. The U.S. faces a potential invasion unprecedented in organized crime annals. Tens of thousands of dedicated gangsters in more than fifty Triads will soon leave Hong Kong. Annual profits from drugs, gambling, extortion, murder for hire, and prostitution are in the billions. The Triads have sophisticated crime networks with international banking and money laundering facilities. All of this will be pitted against U.S. law enforcement agencies that have very few Chinese officers and virtually no understanding of the methods employed by the Triads.

"We have only seen the tip of the iceberg," said a police officer familiar with the Triads. "The Chinese have the potential of making the Mafia in America look like a fraternity of wimps." Unfortunately, he may be right. Already, as honest and industrious Chinese citizens like David W. report, the Triads are spreading a network of violence and fear in the Asian communities. Now their control of the heroin trade is affecting non-Asian neighborhoods as well. If they remain unchecked, their vision of success in the American dream could turn into a nightmare for the rest of us.

Dirt:

From Kazan to Tashkent

● Leningrad
● Helsinki
Oslo   ● Stockholm

Moscow ●   Kazan ●

Warsaw ●

Kiev ●

Volgograd ●
Odessa

Black Sea
Istanbul   Tashkent ●

Dmitrii Likhanov

Athens●

Kabul ●

● Tripoli   Baghdad

Dmitrii Likhanov attended the School of Journalism at Moscow State University. A Soviet journalist for the last ten years, he has been published in a number of international publications, including *Ogonyok*, *El Pais*, and the *London Sunday Times*. He is the author of three books on crime.

The following selection is an excerpt from the book on which he is currently working, *Inside the Soviet Mafia*.

Mr. Likhanov is the publisher of the Russian-language monthly *Top Secret*, one of the most widely distributed *perestroika* publications in the Soviet Union. He lives in Moscow.

W*e in the West have been brought up believing that police states excel at one thing: control of the populace. In particular, the notorious effectiveness of the KGB and the other internal security organs of the USSR is such that the notion of a thriving Soviet criminal underworld barely seems credible. And yet this alternative society, comprising both organized crime and the more loosely organized street gangs, has held sway over vast segments of Soviet life for decades.*

Investigative reporter Dmitrii Likhanov traveled from Moscow to explore gang activity in Kazan and Tashkent, two urban centers separated by a distance of 2,200 miles. Following is his report.

Kazan. I was visiting the regional offices of the Criminal Investigation Unit, the arm of the Soviet Ministry for Internal Affairs (MVD) charged with coordinating anti-gang activities in the area. The deputy director of the unit was a retired schoolteacher named Savelii Tesis. He laid out the basics to me.

"Each gang is formed along the same principles," he explained. "Twelve- and fourteen-year-old boys belong to what's known as the 'husk.' As they grow older they become 'supers,' then 'juveniles,' and when they turn eighteen they are known as 'elders.' Naturally, each gang has a boss."

I told him that while in Kazan I hoped to have a private meeting with the leader of a local gang known as Dirt, and that I had already been awaiting a telephone call from the boss for several days. Tesis frowned and warned me that meeting one-on-one with the leader of one of Kazan's most powerful gangs was extremely risky, and added that even if the meeting should take place, it was unlikely that the boss would actually divulge any information.

"But in all probability," the deputy director remarked, "he simply won't get in touch with you."

A few days later I received a call at my hotel. The boss— or perhaps one of his adjutants or bodyguards, it did not matter—was on the line.

"When can we meet?" I asked.

"Do you know the Pobeda Theater? It's near your hotel," he said. "Be at the bus stop there at five o'clock sharp." He hung up abruptly.

It was dark when the gang leader pulled up to the curb behind the wheel of a sleek Lada of recent vintage, evidence of his status. I slid into the back seat.

Upon closing the door I was overtaken by a powerful wave of Aramis cologne. The boss reeked of it.

"Hi," he said, without turning around.

We dashed through some unfamiliar streets, driving into empty lots and then back out again into the poorly lit Kazan streets. We drove in silence for several minutes. I noticed that all available surfaces in the interior of the car were pasted up with glossy advertisements and pictures from magazines. The stick shift knob was molded in the form of a smiling macaw. The boss himself was dressed in the latest criminal fashion: wool jogging suit and black leather jacket. I couldn't help but think that his taste was foppish.

We finally pulled over in the middle of an abandoned block and he shut off the engine.

"If we had a tail," said the boss, looking at me through the rear-view mirror, "we lost them. Now we can talk."

"In all likelihood we'll never see each other again," I said. "Tell me about yourself. Be honest. What sort of man are you?"

"I don't know," he answered. "You're the first person who's ever asked."

He told me that the quarter in which we were sitting is known locally as Dirt. I asked him why. "There is a lot of dirt here," he said, gesturing outside toward the vacant lots. He had grown up a few blocks from here, he added, in a complex of concrete apartment buildings. The neighborhood was notable only for its alcoholism, lies, distrust, and the regular sour smell of vomit in the hallways of his building. It nauseated him. Most of the residents of this quarter don't notice the dirt much anymore, he said. They live tedious, unsatisfying lives that are nonetheless so demanding that they have little energy to press for better conditions. They get up at dawn and run out the door; work in nearby factories all day; stand in line for meat after work; and return to their dingy, shabby apartments to prepare dinner and sleep. Tomorrow everything will simply be repeated.

The boss did not want to live like that. He and his friends in the neighborhood had stuck together, gathering in an empty courtyard. For them, the courtyard was a place of self-determination and friendship; they were reluctant to return home. That was the provenance of the gang: a desire for something better. They adopted the name of their neighborhood, Dirt.

During their first fight with a gang from the 42nd Quarter, he recalled, he had hammered everyone in his path with a lead pipe and had managed to bring his boys out of the enemy circle while carrying a wounded member on his back. On that day, he unquestionably became boss.

But that was a long time ago, he said. Now he doesn't run at the front of his gang. Instead he drives around the city in a nice car.

The boss had powerful shoulders and a strong build. I asked him about it. He practiced boxing, he said; he had a good body punch and uppercut. He had taught these moves to his boys.

He added that he has a strong antipathy for hippies, punks, heavy metal fans, and communists. He doesn't smoke, drink, or take drugs. He has become a good Muslim. In the morning he likes to take a long bath, first in hot water then in cold. In the evening, he reads from the Koran, peering through the window toward Mecca.

He recently opened a small independent firm and while he didn't describe the business, he did volunteer that every month he sends part of his income to the jails and camps where friends are doing time. He remembers less and less about his gang's violence; but sometimes, he admitted, he is haunted by dreams of the victims' disfigured, bleeding faces whispering to him, and he wakes up in a cold sweat. On those nights a dose of strong coffee helps him stay awake until dawn.

But his skin, hair, and mouth always seem to exude the stench of carrion, he said. Only Aramis can block this penetrating smell. It also helps to attract beautiful women, he added, smiling.

"I don't know what to do," the boss said, shoving a stick of green chewing gum into his mouth. "This gang war started without me. It will probably end without me. This war is one big pain in the ass."

Kazan. The jail cell in which I am standing is narrow and dark. The door creaks closed behind me and I hear a key engage the lock. As I sit down on a bench, footsteps and the jingling of keys recede down the corridor. Somewhere in the distance inmates are laughing and swearing.

Although he is eighteen, the boy seated on the bed opposite me looks like a seventh-grader. He is small, unattractive, and baby-faced. Could it be that he hasn't even started shaving? I wonder. If it were not for his black prison overalls and shaved head, I would think that his presence here was a mistake.

I had leafed through his file, however, acquainting myself with the details of his case. Jura was a murderer. As we sat together, he described the circumstances of the killing.

That past winter, he said, he and his gang were walking to the funeral of a member of a friendly gang when they bumped into a rival gang. It is difficult to say why the fight started, Jura said, who ordered the attack, but it happened. Chunks of ice, feet, hands, and steel balls immediately went into action The other gang started to retreat. Caught up in the fury of the fight, Jura raced after them and clubbed one of the members over the head with a steel pipe. The boy fell. Everyone scattered. The victim lay alone on the ground, reddening the March snow. Several minutes later, safely hidden, Jura heard an ambulance siren wailing in the distance.

Jura told me that initially he had not known the outcome of the fight. When he got home that night, his parents told him that some bastard had killed a boy in the neighborhood. He went to bed but couldn't sleep. He tossed and turned, got up, switched on the light, turned it off again. At two a.m. he finally fell asleep. Later that morning, he said, the police came looking for him.

Sitting in the cell with his file in hand, he thumbed through the material and stumbled across the neatly typed conclusion of the forensic report. He read it, and looked at photographs of the body. Now, months later, he still could not believe that he had killed a man. It was as if he had not even been there that March morning. When he finally looked up from the file, I asked him:

"How did you feel when you struck him? Do you remember?"

"Not very well. But it seems to me I hated them all."

Tashkent. It was a hot Saturday at the hour of afternoon prayer. An elderly Uzbek ran his palms along his face, which was like brown parchment beneath his white turban, and bowed to distant Mecca. Around him in the Eastern bazaar a thousand voices haggled, laughed, exchanged news. The marketplace smelled of sweat and grilled lamb charred along its edges. A man loudly hawking embroidered skullcaps paused to sip tea from a porcelain cup. Elderly Korean women diced and sold radishes, and colorful dresses on display at clothing stalls billowed in the warm wind coming from the desert. The voice of Michael Jackson could be heard in the distance, his tunes oddly echoed by warbling Arabic songs playing nearby.

I spotted him as he negotiated a course through the noisy crowd. Skinny, small, still a boy, he wore the fashionable Marilyn Monroe T-shirt and gold chain with a golden Muslim crescent described to me on the phone. He approached the agreed meeting place near the shoemaker's stall where I stood waiting.

"Salaam," I said, taking off my sunglasses, my prearranged signal.

The boy looked me up and down without interest, then barely motioned with his head toward a winding labyrinth that led to the old city. I followed.

It was cool there and not as noisy as the bazaar, but there was an unbearable stink of dung. Dirty naked children were jumping into a sewage gutter, trying to mount a lazy black piglet. The piglet squealed and ran to the opposite gutter. The children laughed and chased it. A young woman holding a copper pitcher shuffled past us. I smiled at her. The pitcher jerked in her hands, and she blushed. From far away, a muezzin cried from a minaret. We walked in silence.

"Come in," said the boy finally, opening a green door in a whitewashed wall. We entered a dirty yard filled with old furniture, apples, and roosters. "Excuse me," he said as he closed the door behind us, "but I have to frisk you."

Unceremoniously, he emptied my pockets. A journalist's certificate, a pack of cigarettes, a lighter, a pair of glasses, and several microcassettes and a cassette recorder, on which I was frankly relying today, were all laid out on a scratched tabletop.

"You can bring those with you, except for the tape recorder," the boy said. I tried to conceal my dismay. As I reclaimed my things, he vanished behind the door leading into the house. At that moment I determined that I would remember my conversation with the gang leader and write it up immediately after departing. The boy reappeared and beckoned me with his hand, glancing to confirm that the tape recorder remained behind.

The boy led me to the living room, where his boss sat. He looked different from my conception of the leader of an armed gang. He had gracious manners and wore soft house-slippers. He spoke Russian reasonably well. His glasses had thick lenses, and he sported a Claude Montana shirt under the traditional quilted robe. He sat on a sofa among a multitude of brightly colored pillows and plucked emerald grapes from an enormous cluster.

"What kind of grapes do you prefer, white or black?" Ideologue (for that was his name) asked me, gesturing toward an easy chair.

"Black," I answered, sitting down, "the kind without seeds."

"Hey, bring the guest some 'lady fingers'," he called to the boy. Then he looked me in the eye, waiting. "You wanted to meet with me? I am listening."

He listened attentively, without interrupting, as I spoke of gangs and gang activities in Tashkent. Sometimes he nodded his head in assent. Several times he shut his eyes. At other times he smiled condescendingly with the corners of his mouth. When I had finished, he said slowly:

"Things here are not as simple as you think. Our work, so to speak, is not meant to harm society, but to help it. We

135

make society better, and most important, cleaner. In a moral and spiritual way. We are really the emergency medical technicians of society. We clear our big forest of garbage and dirt."

"Like wolves?"

"Not quite. Wolves attack the weak, the young, those who have strayed from the herd. We attack only the socially sick members of society."

"Sorry, but whom do you mean?" I asked, not understanding.

"Whom? Well, for instance, the director of the meat packing plant, who makes the sausage out of unknown ingredients and sells the real meat at the bazaar. A man like that has to be squeezed. In a merciful fashion. After all, these people are parasites on the body of our socialist government in the most literal way. And who, except the people themselves, can protect the government from this evil?"

"But there's the police, the prosecutor, the KGB," I started to object.

"I don't know about the KGB. But the police, the prosecutor, the local party leaders—they are all dirty with sin themselves. Everyone and everything has been bought and sold over and over again for the longest time. And what corruption! You cannot imagine."

"But you think you can save the country? With robbery, rape, murder . . . Isn't this a cruel way of solving problems?"

"What can one do?" Ideologue said wistfully, putting another grape into his mouth. "At the dawn of the Soviet government, in its early days, there was a slogan: expropriation of the expropriators. Remember?"

"I remember. In other words: Beat the rich."

"That's putting it crudely, but the meaning is the same. Even before that, Comrade Stalin and other revolutionaries robbed the tsarist banks and transferred the money abroad to Comrade Lenin so that the Communist Party could exist in exile. Are you saying that this use of force was not justified? According to your logic, should these fine revolutionaries also be called bandits?"

"They are bandits. If they steal, they are criminals under any regime."

"Well, you know, you are just being anti-Soviet!" said Ideologue, offended. "We obviously don't see eye to eye on this. Comrade Stalin, a bandit? Imagine saying that!"

"But how long will the violence last?" I interrupted. "One, two, ten years?"

"As long as social injustice exists. As long as prostitutes, drug addicts, pimps, and other lowlifes are not extinguished. As long as the honest man cannot breathe freely, the violence will continue, forever. This, if you will, is my statement."

We parted warmly, like friends. And as he saw me to the door, he suddenly exclaimed: "Oh, Highest Allah, you didn't even try the grapes."

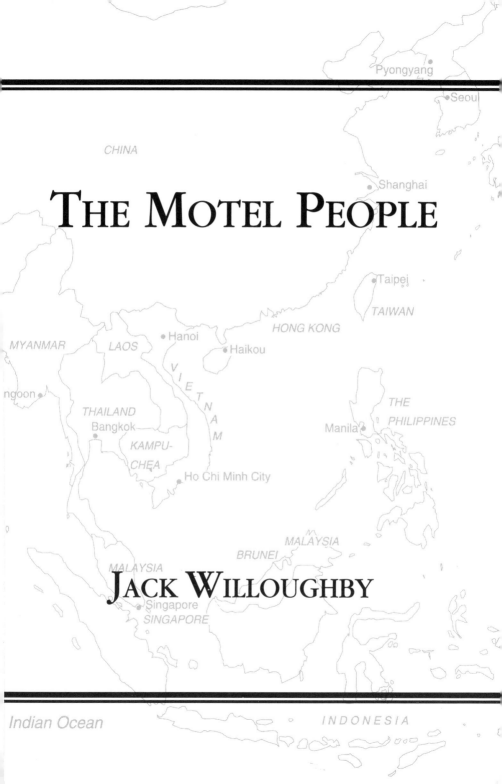

THE MOTEL PEOPLE

JACK WILLOUGHBY

Sergeant Jack Willoughby was born in Louisiana in 1942. In the early 1960s he began working for the United States Army Security Agency.

For the last twenty years Sergeant Willoughby has been a member of the New Orleans Police Department. Since 1982 he has focused his efforts on Asian crime and has become an authority on Asian youth gangs. He is currently Vice President of the International Association of Asian Crime Investigators. He has traveled throughout Southeast Asia, Japan, and the Pacific islands and has lectured extensively on Asian gangs.

Sergeant Willoughby lives in New Orleans with his wife, Judy.

T hey are called by many names: Nomads, Casual Gangs, Pickup Gangs, and Motel People. They range in age from eleven years to about twenty-five. They have one thing in common: They are no longer part of the traditional Vietnamese family structure. Their only true family is the gang.

These ruthless young men and women prey on Vietnamese communities throughout the United States. They forcibly enter homes in the middle of the night to torture, rob, and kill. For a people whose legends tell them that they are descended from a dragon and an angel, the dragon genes seem to have come to the fore in their young lives.

Vietnam has been the scene of conflict since 101 B.C. when it was first invaded by the Chinese. In the ensuing years its people have fought with just about everybody: the Chinese, the French, the Japanese, the Americans, and themselves. Indigenous and foreign rulers have come and gone and borders have expanded and contracted accordingly.

Rebellions involving Vietnamese regional rulers and their Chinese overlords were almost continuous. Sometimes these were large-scale rebellions, sometimes small and almost unnoticed. But the Vietnamese fought, and fought well. In the mid-1800s a French army officer remarked, "They have nothing to fight with, but they fight like tigers."

Not surprisingly, Vietnamese villagers viewed each new regime as temporary, corrupt, and having little concern for or involvement with the governed. The only constant was the neighbors in one's village and one's family. In Vietnam, family was everything. It served as social club, support group, food cooperative, old age pension, and business and planning council. Life without this all-encompassing family network was inconceivable to the average Vietnamese. The result was that Vietnamese villagers depended on their immediate community to solve their problems. Outsiders from another country or even from another village were viewed as potential plunderers. The French colonialists who arrived in the 1800s were not to be trusted. When the Americans came, they were viewed as "the new French."

American military personnel serving in Vietnam did not understand the Vietnamese villager, who in turn did not know why the Americans were there. The villagers were caught in the middle, wedged between the government of South Vietnam, the Americans, who supported it, and the Communist forces of North Vietnam. Each faction would say, "We want to help you," and then the village would be torn apart and the people forced to move. Like other wars, this war affected the people of the land most of all.

In 1975, after most of their American allies had left the country, the Saigon government was defeated by the forces of the Communist north. Over a hundred thousand Vietnamese fled the country, and many more thousands as the years went by.

The first wave of refugees fled, fearing they would be killed by the Communists. This group included many educated Vietnamese and those who had worked with the Americans as well as members of every social group and class. When the hundred thousand-plus refugees came to the United States, they did not understand their new country, nor were they understood. But America took them in.

Immigrant communities settling in America have always experienced trauma as they adjusted to the expectations and language of their adopted land. Immigrants from a particular country historically tended to cluster together in a few places, usually large cities, where their numbers allowed them to maintain their traditions. Several immigrant groups established, or brought with them, gangs: the Sicilian Mafia, the Irish Westies, the Cuban prison gangs. These gangs preyed on members of their own ethnic community and guarded their turf from encroachment by other gangs and ethnic groups.

The Vietnamese came not as immigrants but as refugees. They were widely scattered in communities throughout the United States, wherever sponsoring organizations could be found. Many were held in centralized camps until sponsored and then were sent, somewhat arbitrarily, to their new homes. Few refugees knew what was happening to them because few Americans spoke Vietnamese. The few Vietnamese who spoke English were vastly over-worked.

Families and village communities were further fractured by this dispersal. A family of fishermen from the south might well end up living only one apartment away from strangers from the Central Highlands. This situation might be compared to that of a cotton farmer from Mississippi finding himself next door to a history professor from Colorado. They have different accents and few common interests. This made for neighbors only, not for a cohesive Vietnamese community.

The loss of home, family, livelihood, and traditional support network brought about an increase in alcoholism, child abuse, frustration, and suicide. The refugees brought with them a skepticism toward their own government; this distrust was transferred to the United States government. Moreover, Vietnamese émigrés encountered prejudice from their American neighbors. Most Americans did not understand the trauma they had experienced, their language, or their traditions; some Vietnamese were resented because of their association with a failed war.

143

Many Americans did not understand that they had fought and died along with American soldiers.

A Vietnamese friend of mine was once stopped in a supermarket by an American woman, who shouted at him, "Why are you here? My son was killed in Vietnam! You killed my son and now you're here!"

My friend answered, "Lady, I didn't kill your son. The Communists killed your son. The same people who killed my father in 1968 and my brother in 1972 killed your son. I'm sorry you lost your son, but I didn't do it."

He said the woman gave him a very strange look and walked away. "She didn't understand. I don't blame her for being upset, but it was because she didn't understand anything about the war. I understand. I'm here because we lost."

Some persons already on welfare rolls thought that the Vietnamese, a number of whom were forced to go on welfare, were "taking all the welfare money." There were tales that Vietnamese refugees were given cars, homes, and new boats while poor Americans struggled. Some Americans tried to educate themselves about the new citizens in their midst. Many others had no desire to learn.

The difficulties facing refugee teenagers were enormous. Things that their classmates took for granted were, for them, very odd indeed: shopping in a supermarket as opposed to going to a village market each morning to buy fresh food, going somewhere after school rather than home to help with the chores, being called names by people whom one could not understand. The American idea of family was strange. Everyone had a car. While most Vietnamese families have automobiles now, that was not so in the beginning. The American school system itself was unfamiliar. The school system in Vietnam was designed by the French, and the approach to learning and the subjects—more classical—were unlike those in the United States.

In time, many Vietnamese students whose parents maintained a strong family structure were among the leaders of their classes. Others were at the bottom of the rolls, often those whose families were split apart by the war and the flight from Vietnam. Not many were found in the middle range.

Many of these refugee teenagers also had problems at home. The father was often forced to work at a low-paying job much different than the one he had held in Vietnam: Teachers were reduced to working as janitors, former army colonels to clerking in grocery stores. Moreover, some former military and political figures thought that America had gone back on its word to support the war. The ensuing frustration, coupled with the stresses of leaving their homeland, often severed parents from their children; the adults were too preoccupied with survival to care about much else. Teens were often taught that the family in America had to "do without" in order to support family members left in Vietnam. The adult's ties with the old were, and are, much stronger than the child's.

Vietnamese children were told by their parents to stay away from trouble and, likewise, to stay away from the authorities. One could not trust the government in Vietnam; why should this place be any different? There is no telling what trouble the authorities can make, especially in a strange country.

Children growing up in this mixed environment had to cope with two sets of expectations, that of their parents and that of their new society. Even if the parents were not at home to teach the children proper behavior, they expected the children to exhibit such behavior. The parents did not remember being taught how to behave; it "just happened." They assumed that it would "just happen" to their children also.

Meanwhile, the children in school were exposed to cultural examples of American families. They were somehow expected to resolve the clash of the two cultures, to be properly cultured Vietnamese children and to be Americans, to fit in everywhere, all without help. The miracle is that so many refugee children made it at all. Understandably, some of the children adopted the worst of both cultures. Socially awkward in an English-speaking world, lacking a family network, usually economically strapped, and unable to fit in with peer groups in American society, they sought out others like themselves in order to survive.

Additionally, some of the children who fled Vietnam did so without their families. They were entrusted to friends or associates by their parents, who stayed behind. Often there was no one to care for them; those who brought them to America were too busy with their own family. These children were left to survive on their own. Denied traditional family support and finding little or no acceptance at school, some looked elsewhere. They formed the first traveling gangs.

The young delinquents soon realized that if they moved from community to community, victimizing other Vietnamese, the American authorities would have little idea of how to find them. They did this with the help of their elders.

Included in the first wave of Vietnamese refugees were various adult members of the criminal element. As soon as they arrived they started up their old business: crime. These local criminals became way stations for the young traveling gang members. They advised the gangs of good targets and gave them minor employment in their criminal schemes. They used the teenagers as guards at gambling games, as strong-arms and enforcers.

Vietnamese gangs began to appear around the country, traveling, recruiting, and gaining in numbers. Their growth was fueled by the exodus of the "boat people" who fled Vietnam in small, often unsafe, vessels. At the mercy of wave, wind, and tide, the boat people were also attacked by Thai pirates, who raped, robbed, and killed many of them. Those who survived were taken to refugee camps in Thailand, Malaysia, or the Philippines, where they discovered that the international aid administrators ran the camps only in the daytime. The nights belonged to the gangs. Life consisted of survival. To survive was right, anything else was wrong.

Many ethnic Chinese also fled Vietnam at this time. They did not fit in with the ethnic Vietnamese already assimilated here and were ridiculed by both American and Vietnamese children at school. Some of them joined the young traveling gangs. Others, because of their Chinese ethnicity, attached themselves to already established Chinese gangs—such as the Flying Dragons and Ghost Shadows in New York, the Ping-On in Boston, and the Wa-Ching in California. These young would-be gangsters learned that quick violence is respected and feared. They also learned extortion, robbery, methods of murder, and other criminal stocks in trade from their older mentors.

In 1980 investigators estimated the number of traveling gang members to be in the high hundreds. In 1991 the estimate is in the thousands and growing every day. The majority of the members are runaways. Amerasian children who grew up on the streets of Saigon and other Vietnamese cities have recently swelled their ranks. These fatherless children were treated like dirt because they were half American and often the children of prostitutes. They learned survival on tough streets where, as in the camps, survival was the only game in town.

Petty crime, and major crime when possible, was a way of life, the only way open to them. They may have blond hair or ebony skin, but they speak Vietnamese and think like Asians. These children have not been truly accepted either by their American classmates or their Vietnamese counterparts in neighborhoods or schools. They are, however, accepted by the gangs.

The prime word again is *survival* for the Vietnamese gangs. There are various kinds of gangs, but the traveling gangs are most prominent. They are unlike other gangs in the United States in that they are highly mobile and unconcerned with turf—they don't "belong," they have no home turf to defend. They are highly adaptable.

The traveling gangs exist in cars, motels, and "crash pads." They often travel in carloads of eight or more. Gang members move between Vietnamese communities, staying in one location for weeks, days, or hours, then moving on to another motel in another city. William Cassidy, a private investigator from California and one of the most knowledgeable persons in the United States on Vietnamese crime, especially currency transfers and economic matters, has termed them "the Motel People."

Unlike more traditional gangs, the members of a traveling gang can easily blend with members of other Vietnamese gangs and regroup quickly. Holding no formal gang structure, no formal "membership," they move between cities and communities like fish through water. As they move from city to city they look for prospective members; the disaffected and the unhappy, children like themselves. They offer freedom from adult control and acceptance by the group, in effect a new "family." However, these young gangsters quickly spot someone who claims to be a gangster but is not. The newcomer does not have the proper slang, the proper attitude, nor is he willing to commit any crime required of him in order to belong.

Living in a motel room with twenty others, sleeping in a pile on the floor, constantly moving around the country in stolen cars, are accepted as normal. Survival is everything, fear is a constant companion: not fear of dying, but fear of being captured by the police and placed in prison or a juvenile home where they will lose their independence, be subjected again to a rigid life-style. Maybe even worse, having to go back to their families, where they will never be trusted again but be bound by even more "rules" than before.

A Vietnamese gang member becomes part of a network of gang members throughout the United States, traveling and trading stories and crime tips, recommending motels, passing on names and phone numbers of "safe houses" and of other members in farflung parts of the country.

Gang life quickly removes all moral brakes from new members except the need to be loyal to the gang. They quickly learn that they no longer fit into the normal Vietnamese community, that they are beyond the limits and controls of society. They are told by other gangsters that they are nothing without the gang.

Gang members who formerly felt rejected by a society within which they could not find a place, now capitalize on the fact that they are free of its constraints. They are, in effect, trying to create their own society. They have their own slang: *mo,* for motel, *Cali* for California, a *jump* for a major crime, *Los* for Los Angeles, *the box* for jail. Additionally, they often execute crimes for adult Vietnamese gangsters or alternatively for Vietnamese who are *not* gangsters but who have a grudge against another community member for business or personal reasons. These affiliations broaden the gang's network of contacts, provide them with some protection as well as income, and create a support system. They are feared and notorious in the Vietnamese community for their violent behavior. They are aware of this reputation and use it to intimidate and victimize other refugees.

Gang members, like their more stable elders, are often very intelligent. They work hard at being criminals. They exist by criminal means, either working entirely in their own interest—car theft, robbery, burglary, simple theft—or acting for more experienced criminals in the Vietnamese community as guards at illegal gambling operations, extortionists, strong-arm collectors. The major crimes— drug dealing, bookmaking and sports betting, gold smuggling—are in the hands of the adult criminal. Themselves from refugee families, the gang members are familiar with the predilections of other refugee families and know how to exploit them. For instance, many refugees feel that their assets are safer in the home. They do not trust banks, and at least if the money stays home, in cash or in gold, the tax man cannot get at it. For that reason the "home invasion robbery" is a standard operation for gangsters in the Vietnamese community.

A group of three to ten gang members move into a new city, a new Asian community, find others like themselves, and become friends. They then ask for information about targets, persons who are believed to have money. If there is no evident Vietnamese community, they look in the phone book for Vietnamese surnames. They may even scout for themselves: find a prosperous looking business and follow the owner or his family to their home and observe their habits for hours or even days. When several family members are observed to be at home, they gain entry to the home, either by subterfuge—knocking on the door to ask a question and then rushing in—or by force, kicking in the door. They tie up the family with wire or duct tape and begin a search for valuables. The head-of-household is asked for the location of the hidden valuables. If he does not disclose it violence quickly follows.

The gangs commit particularly cruel acts of violence— including scalding, beating, and rape—which are usually inflicted on the more vulnerable members of the family such as grandmothers, infants, and wives. Males are forced to watch as other family members are abused. Few can watch such things without giving in and revealing the location of the hidden valuables. The young gangsters have no conscience; they do what they need to do to get what they want.

Armed robberies of businesses are also frequent. With few exceptions, the targets are Vietnamese-owned stores. Most robberies are well planned. A store is cased by the traveling gang members who have recently arrived or by local gang members. They know who owns the store, how many people operate the business, and where to look for valuables. They try to make their move when no customers are present. As with home invasion robberies, the gang often tie up the owner of the store and brutally abuse one or more of the employees to learn where additional money or valuables are stashed. Victims are threatened that if they call the police the gang will be back.

Auto theft is another gang specialty. They make their own master keys by cleverly manipulating a regular car key. Gangs often find another car of the same make and model and exchange license plates with that car to eliminate the danger of an officer casually checking the license plate and finding that the car has been stolen. They run a stolen car until it breaks down and then steal another one.

Gangs also kidnap people. Police have learned that some female gang members were once kidnap victims. The girls were seized from their home, school, or a teenage hangout and forced into narcotics, sex, and general criminal and gang activity.

These words are from a diary of a young Vietnamese girl who fled a crash pad after the arrest of several members of her gang:

December 12—We went to the mall. We had a good time. Bobby got into a fight and we had to leave.
December 17—I'm in Houston.

December 18—We went to the mall and hung around. I went shopping with some money Bobby gave me. I had my hair done. We had a good time.

December 19—Went with Bobby to gamble. We stayed out all night.

December 20—More gambling. Bobby got in a fight and got shot.

January 5—Pensacola is O.K. We went to the mall again and hung around. We went to play pool.

January 7—Phuong said we were going to the mall again and hang around. We went to play pool.

January 10—I wish I could go home. I wish I could go home. I wish I could go home.[*]

Few of these gang members ever make it home, if they have a sense of where home is. Their modus operandi reflects their condition, carrying only false identification or none. If there is one emblem that approximates an idealized sense of self, it is the tattoos they wear to proclaim themselves as gangsters: Dragons and tigers are popular, as are skulls and various swords and knives. The tattoos say to the community at large: "Look at me. Be careful, I'm a criminal. Don't mess with me, just give me what I ask for and you won't get hurt."

For those gang members who are not killed by adversaries or friends, are not sentenced to long prison terms, and don't die from drugs, there is the possibility of integration into a larger form of community: the interconnection of organized crime in this country. Having been trained in the boot camp of alienation, they have gained all the experience they need to excel on the adult level in the brutal practice of their work.

---

[*] I am recalling these words from memory, as I no longer have access to the diary. The last three sentences were underlined twice.

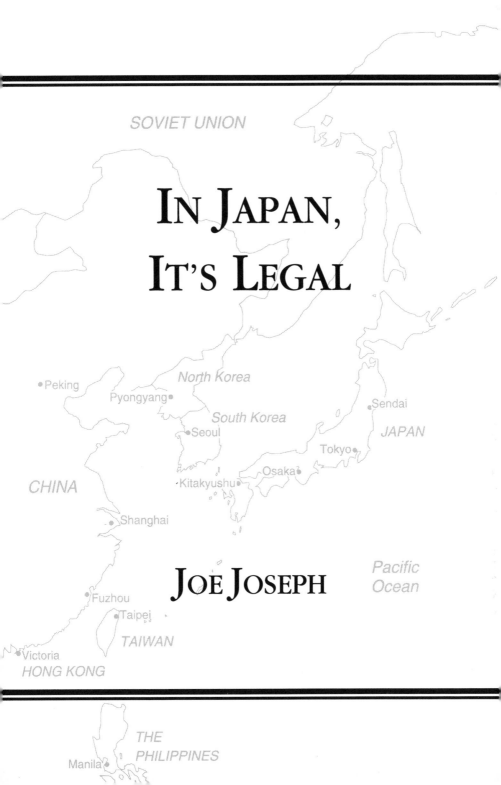

IN JAPAN,
IT'S LEGAL

JOE JOSEPH

Joe Joseph recently returned to England from Japan, where for three years he was Tokyo bureau chief for the *London Times*. During that time he traveled widely throughout Asia. He previously worked as a correspondent for Reuters Information Services, in London and New York. His work has also been featured in several British and American magazines.

Mr. Joseph is now a senior writer for the *London Times* and is currently writing a book on Japan and the Japanese for Viking Penguin. He lives in London with his wife, Jane, and son, Thomas.

For an idea of just how easy it can be to make crime pay in Japan, take an envious glance at the case of Seiichi Kawaguchi. He picked out the names of more than 4,000 rich Japanese at random—not all that tricky in a country where people buy a new Rolex with their spare change and have to save for, oh, a couple of months at least to pay for a shiny red Mercedes convertible—and then sent them blackmail letters threatening to expose their guilty secrets.

He hit the jackpot—well, a decent enough jackpot for a job that didn't require much more than gall, a sharp pen, and a Tokyo telephone directory.

By the time police tracked him down, Kawaguchi had already picked up five million yen from over 130 people who could not rest on their *futons* at night for fear that their extramarital affairs, graft, medical malpractices, and other dirty deeds were about to be exposed. Some Japanese might not be all that surprised by Kawaguchi's success: Japan is so overcrowded that it is possible to commit five blackmailable offenses just getting off a subway train. Even so, the cheek of the scam is breathtaking. "Even though I had no proof at all, I hit on a lot of people with a guilty secret," the 48-year old Kawaguchi told police when he was finally caught. Business was so brisk that Kawaguchi had to hire part-time help to address and put stamps on his blackmail letters.

Kawaguchi is not even a member of the *yakuza,* Japan's famous organized crime syndicates, which have turned large-scale extortion into just another inventive fund-raising scheme. Japanese police reckon that nearly one in three Japanese businesses pays up when *yakuza* racketeers come knocking on the executive suite door asking for cash. Sometimes these "donations" are as much as a million dollars, which is an awful lot of money for, say, a phony newsletter that the gangster might offer in return, just for appearances' sake. The more sophisticated hoods turn up at annual shareholders' meetings and threaten to disrupt the proceedings or to expose embarrassing details about the company's bookkeeping or the president's bedmates.

Such nimble racketeering makes the crooks in "Kojak" look rather heavy-handed. But now Tokyo is bracing for a more clumsy gangland war as Japan's biggest crime syndicate tries to spread its wings and swoop on the capital, a rival's lucrative turf. Police are in a panic. They are worried that shoot-outs that have cracked the calm of other big cities may be on their way to Tokyo. That would bring a peculiar sense of threat to a city where women roam freely after dark and where even pickpocketing is rare.

But the mammoth *yamaguchi-gumi* gang, which is running out of opportunities in its home base in Kobe, a busy port in western Japan, is not coming to Tokyo purely to hawk loans and hookers. It has just come to light that the gang, far and away Japan's largest, is also a huge investor on the Tokyo stock market, which—until Japanese share prices started sinking faster than a thermometer stuck into a snowdrift, was more reliably rewarding than gambling or drugs.

A new rule that has just been made by Japan's finance ministry requires anyone holding more than five percent of a company's shares to declare his stake. This is common practice in most Western nations but a novelty in Japan, where the Dickensian level of corporate secrecy would make New York's more imaginative stock arbitrageurs green with envy. The result is that Japanese boardrooms are suddenly frantic to discover whether mobs are on their share registers too, after it was discovered that the *yamaguchi* syndicate is the biggest shareholder in a large and well-known textile company. The gang has built up a stake worth 20.5 billion yen in the firm. Police haven't a clue whether the mob is just investing or laundering dirty profits.

In a rare crackdown on organized crime, police raided *yamaguchi-gumi* offices last October after a spate of shootouts between rival gangs in Osaka, Kobe's neighbor. Police have traditionally turned a blind eye to underworld activities as long as mobsters refrained from settling rivalries in the streets and visited their mothers at new year (the mobsters' mothers, not the police's). But a younger generation of gang bosses seems less finicky about keeping a low profile when the rewards can be so high. Police fear that Tokyo will be the next battleground. They say the *yamaguchi-gumi* is inviting trouble by breaking a secret pact not to trespass on the Tokyo mobsters' territory.

As one of Tokyo's long-time gangsters put it: "The *yamaguchi-gumi* has disturbed the prosperous coexistence of local syndicates in Tokyo. We must take action." He may make it sound like mopping up a small milk spill at a ladies' coffee hour. But when the Japanese take someone on, they approach the job very seriously. Ask Detroit.

According to a senior Tokyo police official who tracks gang activity: "The *yamaguchi-gumi* has opened more than forty offices in Tokyo over the past year. Tokyo is the center of the Japanese economy, and the *yamaguchi-gumi* has expanded as much as it can in western Japan and other parts of the country where it is strong, so they have to come here. They go at night to bars and the like to pass out their name cards, which is a code for seeking protection money."

Japan is a country where even your doorman swaps business cards. If you come home at night without at least fifteen new name cards in your wallet, most Japanese will think you have spent the day in social purdah. So be wary next time a thuggish looking man with maybe the end of a finger missing (a common sacrifice made by younger gangsters needing to show repentance to the boss),hands you his card. And think carefully before handing him your own.

There are nearly 90,000 *yakuza* members, famous for their tattooed bodies, tightly permed hair, flashy white suits, and big limousines. Even at a conservative guess, organized crime is a $10 billion a year business in Japan. That is almost $120,000 per gang member, or nearly four times what the average Japanese office worker earns a year. Although they make up only one tenth of one percent of Japan's population, the *yakuza* have a wide reach. At least one quarter of all homicide arrests and two thirds of extortion-related arrests involve *yakuza* gang members. Selling drugs, running illegal gambling dens, making book illegally on bicycle and horse racing, lending their muscle (literally) to bigwig occasions, smuggling arms—all these services are available from your local *yakuza* franchise. When those streams of income run dry, *yakuza* gangsters are not averse to marching into a stockbroker's office and declaring that they have been sold shares that fell in price and that the stockbroker had better buy them back at the purchase price.

As money becomes harder to come by, competition between syndicates swells. And as the turf wars between rival gangs grow, both the police and the victims of gangsters' mischief are beginning to tire of the old saw that organized crime is at least better than disorganized crime.

Top bananas of the *yamaguchi-gumi* were driven recently in a convoy of twenty luxury limos to a Yokohama restaurant to discuss strategy for expanding their operations in Tokyo. The gang has about 30,000 members, but only a paltry 500 of them in Tokyo. One senior member of the gang told a reporter for Japan's *Yomiuri*, Japan's biggest-selling daily newspaper, "We can absorb smaller syndicates in local areas. But it's difficult to do that in Tokyo, where all the smaller syndicates are affiliated with larger organizations. So we have poured into Tokyo so that the *yamaguchi-gumi* can take root here by itself."

Oh, dear.

The syndicate's headquarters in Kobe gives five million to ten million yen to gang members to set up new "business offices" in Tokyo. It may sound peculiar to you or me, but being a gang member is legal in Japan, and most hoods wear lapel badges stating their affiliation and exchange business cards that denote their rank. But in Tokyo the *yamaguchi-gumi* are trying to stay discreet. The seed-corn money from HQ covers start-up costs. Once the office is running, it sends at least 300,000 yen a month back to base.

Nevertheless, you can't stroll around town dropping quietly threatening business cards unless you have a lot of eager youngsters to do the dropping. So the syndicate is recruiting new members in Tokyo. "We approach people who hang out in bars," says one member. "We buy them a sharp suit or something like that and say, 'Hey, you look great in that suit. Why don't you come and work with us?' They follow." They may well follow because they are in a state of shock. In Japan new recruits to the country's fussier employers, such as banks and car makers, may have to spend a few weeks polishing their bosses' shoes or singing "My Way" in the local shopping mall to build self-confidence before being fully embraced by their new workmates. Merely accepting a new suit, without any shoe-shining or public crooning, may well be too tempting to resist. The recruits earn a regular monthly salary of 150,000 to 200,000 yen, just as if they had been hired by Mitsubishi or Toyota. And they get a lapel pin.

The gangs that control Tokyo are not happy about their rival's expansion plans. They are building a war chest to defend their patch. "We have raised more than 100 million yen," says a member of the heavyweight, Tokyo-based *sumiyoshi rengokai* gang. "We can keep fighting for at least six months with this money. We have one gun for every three men. We send young members to the Philippines for shooting practice."

There is recession and unemployment in the West, and a job is a job. Does this sound like just the sort of work you have been looking for? But reflect a little before you pack your bags and start practicing with your chopsticks. It may sound up your street. But not everyone is suited. Here's a short questionnaire that might give you an inkling whether a career in the *yakuza* is really for you.

Answer the following questions:

1. Next to my skin I most like the feel of
   a. a silk kimono
   b. scented massage oil
   c. tattoo ink
2. In my spare time I like to run
   a. the marathon
   b. stalls at charity bazaars
   c. stimulant drugs
3. When I have a bit of spare cash I have a weakness for
   a. going to the theater
   b. buying a few CDs
   c. lending it short term at 35 percent a week
4. When I'm really upset about something I tend to
   a. take a long soak in a hot tub
   b. call my therapist
   c. take out a contract on someone
5. On seeing an aggressive-looking youth, my first instinct is to
   a. cross to the other side of the street
   b. knock him down a peg or two
   c. initiate him into my gang

6. To show respect, I think people should
    a. bow deeply
    b. roll out the red carpet
    c. cut off their little finger as a token sacrifice
7. The most important asset a man could own is
    a. a portable telephone
    b. a yacht
    c. the Osaka police force
8. When I see my boss in a bar with his secretary, I feel my social duty is to
    a. look the other way
    b. join them for a drink
    c. blackmail him

How did you get on?

Bibliography

Burgess, Anthony. *A Clockwork Orange.* New York: W.W. Norton, 1963. The classic novel-turned-film is perhaps one of the most grisly fictional depictions of violent hooliganism.

Campbell, Anne. The Girls in the Gang: A Report From New York City. New York: Basil Blackwell, 1984. The author spent six months with each of three gangs in New York City getting a perspective on Black, Latino, and White gangs there.

Forbes, George and Paddy Meehan. *Such Bad Company.* Edinburgh: Paul Harris Publishing, 1982. The authors present a history of Glasgow's more unseemly residents. Their lives are, they argue, as much a part of the city's history as any other residents' but haven't received enough attention.

Gardner, Sandra. *Street Gangs.* New York: Franklin Watts, 1983. An investigation of gangs in cities and suburbs, including the reasons for gang violence, and ways some communities have tried to tackle gang problems.

Haskins, James. *Street Gangs: Yesterday and Today.* New York: Hastings House, 1974. Hoskins traces American street gangs (especially gangs of immigrants) in New York City from the early 1800s to the mid-1970s. He argues that discrimination and a need to belong were and still are major factors in pushing youth into gangs.

Hoenig, Gary. *Reaper: The Story of a Gang Leader.* Indianapolis: Bobbs-Merrill, 1975. The author describes a year in the life of a Bronx, New York, gang leader. Hoenig attempts to determine what drove this youth, and others like him, into gangs.

Kaplan, David E. and Alec Dubro. *Yakuza: The Explosive Account of Japan's Criminal Underworld.* Reading, MA: Addison-Wesley, 1986. The authors examine the notorious Japanese gangs that deal in drugs, extortion, and guns.

Kelly, Gail Paradise. *From Vietnam to America: A Chronicle of the Vietnamese Immigration to the United States.* Boulder, CO: Westview Press, 1977. The difficult transition from Vietnamese refugee to settled immigrant is discussed in this book. Kelly also puts forward some of the differences between refugees' needs and what the U.S. was willing to offer.

Lyman, Michael D. *Gangland.* Springfield, IL: Charles C. Thomas, 1989. Organized crime is involved in the trafficking of all the drugs that enter the United States. Lyman examines the role of those rackets, including the youth gangs that are responsible for much of the final distribution of the drugs to end users.

Patrick, James. *A Glasgow Gang Observed.* London: Eyre Methuen, 1973. The author writes about his encounters with a Glasgow gang on two occasions in 1966 and 1967. It is a descriptive, rather than analytical, account that does not attempt to analyze the gang situation but rather offers a glimpse of gang life at that time and place.

Posner, Gerald L. *Warlords of Crime—Chinese Secret Societies: The New Mafia.* New York: McGraw-Hill, 1988. Triads, the Chinese secret societies, are responsible for some of the major international crime. This book shows some of their activity in the Far East.

Rosner, Lydia. *The Soviet Way of Crime.* South Hadley, MA: Bergin and Garvey Publishers, 1986. This book examines the criminality of Soviet citizens both in their home country and in the United States. It discusses the rampant institutional corruption in the Soviet Union as well as the crime of recent immigrants from the Soviet Union.

Sale, Richard T. *The Blackstone Rangers: A Reporter's Account of Time Spent With the Street Gang on Chicago's South Side.* New York: Random House, 1971. Based on a series of interviews with members of Chicago's Blackstone Rangers, the book presents the views of gangs held by the members themselves.

Smith, Ernest A. *American Youth Culture.* New York: Free Press of Glencoe, 1962. Discussing the differences between youth culture and adult culture, the author argues that youth culture is passed from one generation to the next.

Taylor, Carl S. *Dangerous Society.* East Lansing: Michigan State University Press, 1990. An investigation of inner-city gangs in Detroit, especially those whose members are very young.

Townsend, Peter. *The Girl in the White Ship: A Story of the Vietnamese Boat People.* London: Collins, 1981. Townsend writes about a girl who was the only survivor of a boatload of fifty refugees who were shipwrecked and marooned on an isolated coral reef.

Webb, Margot. *Coping with Street Gangs.* New York: Rosen Publishing Group, 1990. The author discusses the nature of gangs, how they are organized, what they do and how to avoid being caught up in gang life.

Index